FOLLY COVE

A Smuggler's Tale of the Pot Rebellion

FOLLY COVE
A Smuggler's Tale of the Pot Rebellion

Kermit Schweidel

Cinco Puntos Press
www.cincopuntos.com
EL PASO, TEXAS

FIRST EDITION
10 9 8 7 6 5 4 3 2 1

Library of Congress Cataloging-in-Publication Data

Names: Schweidel, Kermit, author.
Title: Folly Cove : a smuggler's tale of the pot rebellion / by Kermit
  Schweidel.
Description: First edition. | El Paso, Tex. : Cinco Puntos Press, [2017]
Identifiers: LCCN 2017028060 | ISBN 9781941026823 (pbk. : alk. paper)
Subjects: LCSH: Schweidel, Kermit. | Drug dealers—United States—
Biography.
  | Marijuana—United States. | Drug traffic—United States.
Classification: LCC HV5805.S39 A3 2017 | DDC 364.1/77092 [B] —dc23
LC record available at https://lccn.loc.gov/2017028060

Cover design by Scott Crum
Interior design by Bluepanda Design Studio

To Emmy Jean

Who believed in me more than I believed in myself.
And inspired me as only a mother can.

CONFESSIONS OF A CONVICTED FELON

Though the story is true, I have changed the names of several participants who wished to remain anonymous. In some cases, I have composited characters and associated them with events they may not have been part of. The stories themselves are true, but introducing more names would only confuse the narrative. So I took a few liberties in the interest of adding connective tissue without getting tangled in a sea of names. Otherwise, I have stuck to the facts as we recalled them some forty years later. After all that time, I readily admit that our operating systems may have fallen a few upgrades behind. But we still have a shitload of memory. And memories like this are made to last a lifetime.

PROLOGUE
May 1980

A fat roach beckoned from the ashtray. I fired it up, as was my custom on the drive home from work. It was a juicy little remnant that had begun its day a full-grown joint on the morning edition of my commute. Life just seemed to go better with a little buzz on. And at the moment, life was going just fine.

I was employed as a senior copywriter at El Paso's largest ad agency. Mithoff Advertising was a mid-size shop that put a premium on good creative and held tightly to a prestigious roster of regional and local accounts. I had built a nice portfolio in the course of my two-year stint and was earning a surprisingly good living creating thirty- and sixty-second radio and TV commercials, writing print ads and outdoor boards, and cobbling the occasional catalog.

In advertising, all roads lead to major markets. That's where the best brands and biggest budgets reside. And that's where my new wife and I were determined to go. Debbie had been a broadcast producer at the agency where we met and fell in love. Once married, we began to discover the pitfalls of relationships in the workplace. Two voices heard as one might have worked for Simon & Garfunkel, but it was sudden death for a career-minded couple. So I stayed put and Debbie took a job producing for Channel 9, the local NBC affiliate. It was a temporary solution. We were determined to pursue the limits of our uncluttered ambition. Of course, we had no idea where that might take us. But we believed it would be a long way from El Paso, Texas.

It was a pleasant afternoon in the high-desert spring. I was looking ahead to tonight's game. I played fast-pitch softball in a competitive men's league. The games were hotly contested, but never hotly enough to stand in the way of a few cold ones to wash down the residue of the results. It was as much a social occasion as anything else—an evening among friends under the welcoming lights of a neighborhood ballpark. Debbie, who never missed a game, was probably already home packing the cooler.

I pulled off I-10 and headed west into El Paso's upper valley, our little slice of which was a red-brick shoebox in a small clearing of gravel and weeds just a six-iron from the Rio Grande. Two large pecan trees shaded the long, narrow lot. The house sat back about forty-five feet from an irrigation ditch that fronted the property. It was hardly more than a human file cabinet, but the location offered precious shade and scenic relief from the scorched desert landscape. Driving up to our little place on Elmwood Road, I was happy to see Debbie's yellow Volkswagen already in the driveway.

Parked next to the ditch in front of the house, I noticed an unfamiliar sedan, totally generic but for the clear signal of its whip antenna. Side by side in the front seat a pair of casually clad, clean-shaven guys about my own age were conspicuously reading the newspaper. The silent alarm of paranoia began to sound as I was struck by the certainty that despite their apparent interest in current events, they had come in regard to events of the past.

I swung into the drive and heard their engine crank and fire. By the time I rolled to a stop, their sedan had pulled in behind, effectively blocking my retreat. I got out with my hands in plain sight as the two approached cautiously, identifying themselves as agents of the El Paso DEA. My pulse was headed for terminal velocity, but somehow my brain overrode the panic, clearly reciting the mantra from long ago: *Say nothing.*

I expected at any moment to be thrown onto the hood of my Honda, aggressively frisked, and paraded in front of the neighbors in handcuffs. Obviously, these guys hadn't watched as many cop shows as I had. There was no drama, no hostility, no handcuffs—just a cursory pat down by a painfully polite pair of federal agents who kindly suggested we go inside so I might be spared the reading of my rights in front of the neighbors.

Debbie, who stood at the front door struggling to process the sudden death of our dreams, seemed to be searching for any explanation beyond the obvious. I had never concealed the truth of my past, but neither had I gone into much detail. We shared the conviction that our former lives were best left to history. Unfortunately, history had suddenly come calling, hungry for a bite of our future.

For me, the offense in question was a brief but eventful detour from which I had long since retraced my steps. In fact, my arrest came four years and ten months after the alleged crime—just two months shy of the statute of limitations. But ours is a government with a long memory and a longer reach. And my name was etched in consequence at the end of the dreaded phrase, "The United States of America versus…" I was looking at a maximum of fifteen years in the federal penitentiary. I was on my way to the El Paso County Jail, and about to be reunited with some old friends.

The story behind that day is one I have put off telling for nearly forty years. It has always been there, residing quietly on the back burner of my life. I just never seemed to get around to it. No surprise, really. When I look back, I realize it was never my story to tell. It belongs to others who were far bigger stakeholders than I. Some have remained friends for life. Others have drifted away on the prevailing current. Still others have died. But enough of us remain to share the unlikely tale of a loose confederacy of homeboys who chased their first life-altering high from the mountains of Mexico to the desert Southwest; from the growing fields of Sinaloa and the coast of Colombia, all the way to the edge of Massachusetts and a place called Folly Cove. It was there that we endeavored to pull off the most audacious pot smuggle yet attempted.

Folly Cove, however, is not where the tale begins, but the apogee of an arc that originated in a wide-open border town on the forgotten edge of nowhere—El Paso, Texas. Against a 1970s backdrop of Vietnam and Kent State, political corruption and radical activism, this is how a brotherhood of border rats rode the adrenaline high straight to the fast lane of America's Cannabis Road. It is the story of restless youth meeting illicit opportunity at the right time in the perfect place. And it is a story we will tell together, just as we lived it.

PART I

CHASING THE HIGH
1970—1974

Jack Stricklin, ca. 1970

AUTHORITY ISSUES
1970

With the foothills of the Rockies on the horizon and Sandia Peak at his back, Jack Stricklin rolled south through Albuquerque on his way to El Paso. The yellow and white four-wheel drive International Scout hummed along I-25 at a steady pace, its knobby off-road tires whining in protest at the civilized blacktop.

The year was 1970. Jack Stricklin was twenty-five years old, just out of the Navy, and expecting to hook up with a couple of friends who shared his enthusiasm for the commerce of pot. His modest goal was to deal his way to a $10,000 stake. Why that was the figure he had in mind—or what came next—he couldn't tell you. It just felt right. Jack Stricklin was a person who lived instinctively and refused to be burdened by anyone's expectations but his own. At the moment, he was expecting to get high, puffing contentedly on a tightly rolled joint as he rode the white line with carefree indifference.

Jack Stricklin Jr. grew up in a well-to-do family. His father, Jack Sr., was the vice president of El Paso Natural Gas. He had worked his way up from remote outposts and rugged pipelines to become one of the company's top executives. Being his only son came with high expectations. But if anyone thought the junior in his name was going to render him a carbon copy of senior, they didn't know Jack.

I met him for the first time when I was twelve years old. Jack was closer to seventeen, but even then possessed an easy-going charisma that could charm the knickers off Snow White. We had just moved to El Paso, where my father would serve his final tour of duty and retire after thirty years in the Army.

El Paso, Texas was a systemic shock no kid should have to endure. It was dusty, hot, ugly, only marginally civilized, and largely inhabited by people who spoke an alien tongue and ate food so spicy you could taste the flames. We were less than a hundred miles from a location of such desolation that the government selected it as proving ground for their early nukes. Had my father really spent thirty years in the Army and fought in two wars so we could settle down in a skillet and spend a lifetime being sandblasted?

Moving to the desert was one of the big traumas of my young life. Jack Stricklin was a bright spot in that early transition. It was my older sisters, of course, who brought him into my orbit. I was just the kid brother—an irritating little wart all but ignored by the *Sisters from Hell.* But to Jack, I was someone worth getting to know. When he called the house and I answered the phone (a rare occurrence), it was as if he had called just to talk to me. I could always make him laugh. He could always make me feel a little less invisible.

Though Jack Stricklin was a good friend of both my sisters, he hoped to be better friends with one or two of the girls with whom they frequently hung out. Our home on Fort Blvd. was the preferred gathering place, so I became Jack's pipeline to the late-night gabfests that accompanied many a sleepless slumber party. It was our first conspiracy. And the beginning of a connection that would last a lifetime.

Jack Stricklin wasn't known for his common sense, but for his uncommon sense of humor. The purpose of his life was to be amused, and he chased his fun at a full gallop. Though he had little use for details, Jack processed information at warp speed.

He was a cut-to-the-chase guy who relied on his own intuition and ignored conventional wisdom.

Physically, Jack was a presence you could hardly fail to notice, with a larger-than-life personality and a body to match. At 6' 3" he appeared a bit on the wiry side, carrying about 180 pounds, most of which was lean muscle and raw energy. Many of his friends called him *Flaco,* Spanish for skinny. But Jack worked out three or four times a week and ate like a sumo wrestler. He took vitamins and supplements and drank milkshakes for breakfast. Nevertheless, he was forever Flaco. And Flaco burned calories like a greyhound in training.

A shaggy crop of sandy blonde hair fell straight to his shoulders, framing an avian beak that presided over a drooping mustache—an appropriate counterweight for a man who laughed at life with the hair trigger of a cap gun. To Jack, there was no such thing as a bad joke. From the darkest satire to the most ridiculous slapstick, he was a human spasm, erupting in laughter at the slightest provocation.

Jack himself wasn't all that funny. He enabled funny. And in the process attracted friends like fungus to a toenail. If you so much as served him breakfast, you'd be on a first-name basis by the second cup of coffee. There was nothing phony or unnatural about his openness. Jack genuinely liked people, and most people couldn't help but like him back. He was totally free with his friendship. On the flip side, you had to earn his trust.

If you were a friend of Jack Stricklin, you could ask of him nearly any favor. If it were in his power, he was likely to comply. But *tell* Jack what to do and he would chomp the bit so hard, sparks would fly out his ass as he applied the emergency brake with urgent force. Authority was not his friend. He had no time for rules, no patience for structure, and no need for motivation. Jack seized the wheel and hung on for the ride, not caring where it ended up but only what it offered along the way. Most of the time it offered trouble, but even that was something Jack Stricklin never took seriously.

Jack Stricklin

You might say I had issues with authority. It probably started with the Mormon Church and all their ridiculous rules and regulations. I was thirteen years old and the Bishop of the Mormon Church was telling me who I could and couldn't be friends with. He wasn't going to tell me I couldn't hang out with all my non-Mormon friends. All that religious stuff was just silly. I don't like being told what to do. And I can be a stubborn son of a bitch.

High school was a joke. We'd cut class and go to Juarez or down to the river. There was too much fun to be had to sit in a classroom and pretend to be interested. My father and I decided that military school might be a good idea. As much as I hated authority, he and I both knew I would never graduate without a little discipline. And there were way too many distractions in El Paso. I actually kind of liked the idea of going away to school.

Allen Military Academy was a prep school for Texas A&M. Once I got there, I figured out what made the place work. It was so fucking boring you had to study just to break the monotony. It took me two and a half years to make second lieutenant. Usually you made colonel by the time you were a senior. But I raised the art of underachieving to new heights.

I actually graduated on the Dean's List in 1963. That was the last Dean's List I ever saw. After graduation, I came back to El Paso expecting to work for El Paso Natural Gas before I started college in the fall. My father was the vice president. So I'm thinking he's going to get me a cushy job parking cars, and I can hang out and chase girls all summer. But instead he says, "Pack your bags, Jack. You're leaving."

"What?"

"You're going to Farmington."

"Farmington? What am I going to do in Farmington?"

"You're going to work on the pipeline."

The minute he said *work*, I kind of sat up and took notice. "What am I going to do on the pipeline?"

He said, "Oh, there's all kinds of things you can do on the pipeline. I'm sure they'll think of something."

So the next thing I know, my sister Bonnie has got me packed and away we go to Farmington, New Mexico. She helps me find a little apartment and a restaurant that makes lunches for you. She knew I'd starve to death if I didn't have that. So she got it all taken care of, and she left.

The next day I went to jail. That was my first time in jail. A friend had gone with me to Farmington, and we were having a beer party that got a little out of hand. I actually went to jail three times that summer for public intoxication and disorderly conduct. It was ridiculous.

Anyway, I went to work on the pipeline digging ditches with a pick and shovel. It was probably one of the most enjoyable three months I ever spent in my life. I had a girlfriend in Farmington, a car, and a steady paycheck. What more could you want?

Toward the end of that summer, we were in Utah, laying the pipeline across the river, and I was in a ditch, digging out a dogleg. My foreman was working the backhoe with me. It was just the two of us, and he said, "Jack, did you ever hear what your father did after you came up here?"

"What are you talking about?"

"The second week you were here?"

"No. What did he do?"

"He came up here on Thursday, when all you guys were still in the field. He called in all the foremen and told us that if you didn't do your job, we should fire you. And then he said, "If I hear that Jack isn't doing his job and you don't fire him, I will fire him myself. And then I will fire you."

Well, God almighty, no wonder they worked me like a

rented mule. They were more worried about me fucking up than I was. But it was a great summer. I learned a lot about work ethic, and I learned a lot about the pipeline— mainly that I didn't ever want to work on one.

TOUGH GUY
1968

Mike Halliday, ca. 1970

Mike Halliday grew up playing with the big kids. He was the pebble in their shoe. The longer they tried to ignore him, the more irritating he became. Mike ran on a hi-octane blend of perpetual energy, with mind and body constantly colliding in a non-stop demolition derby. It was as if all the shiny objects were put on the earth just to distract him. He bounced off his life like a rubber ball.

Mike Halliday was determined to run with the big dogs, even if it meant suffering the occasional bite. If they wanted to fight, he would fight. If they wanted to drink, he would drink. If they wanted to party in Juarez, he was more than happy to oblige. About the only thing Mike wouldn't do is back down. The occasional pummeling might not have made him any the wiser, but it instilled an enduring toughness that would ultimately earn him the acceptance of the older boys.

Mike, of course, would tell you he won more fights than he lost. But the mangled claw that was his right hand, the semi-wayward nose and picket-fence smile might lead one to seriously reconsider the definition of winning. He was a solidly built 5' 7" of strutting bantam, with curly hair, slightly bowed legs, and a strong chin that preceded him wherever he went. There was about him an aura of mischief that was both innocent and foreboding. Sober, he was a bright, engaging, quick-witted guy with a wicked sense of humor and an innate curiosity. Drunk, he was a little ball of hate.

Mike had grown up the son of a warrior, patriot and disciplinarian. His father was a lieutenant colonel who wore his rank comfortably, in or out of uniform. Growing up the first son of a career soldier, in fact, was something Mike and I had in common. My own father was a retired lieutenant colonel and West Point graduate who ruled his family with military precision.

Survivors of both the Great Depression and World War II, these were men who cast long shadows. The rules of the road were absolute. As a son, you could either embrace the rigid measure to which you were held, or rebel and incur the wrath of the righteous soldier. For Mike it was an easy choice. He was not his father's son. He was his father's problem. And he would express himself by being everything his father was not.

Among the things Mike Halliday was not, *successful student* would be listed near the top. He could hardly sit still through a Saturday matinee, much less a spirited reading of *Canterbury Tales*. If you wanted him to find the hypotenuse of a triangle, why couldn't he just get up and look for it? And how in the hell does the ability to parse a sentence make you a better person?

To his credit, Mike managed to complete four years of high school. Unfortunately, four years were not nearly enough to earn him a diploma. At the age of eighteen, Mike Halliday applied the holy trinity of ways to fuck up your life: he dropped out of high school, got married, and had a baby. It might not make him the *Most Likely to Succeed*, but it would earn him a draft deferment and keep him out of Vietnam.

It should be noted that Mike was not a stupid kid. He may have been an undiagnosed alphabet of learning disabilities, but when something did manage to attract his interest, it was in for a thorough examination. What held Mike's attention were all things mechanical, the early manifestation of which resulted in all things being taken apart. It wasn't that he was so curious about how they'd been put together. He knew that instinctively. Taking things apart simply allowed him to find a better way to put them back together—with a few custom alterations that were often an improvement, occasionally a disaster.

When Mike and I sat down to begin this book, we were gathered around the workbench in his eastside El Paso shop, a windowless warehouse with a fifteen-foot ceiling and concrete floor. Without using a single watt of electricity, the place was lit up like the Rose Bowl on game night. Thanks to a unique set of tubular skylights on which he held patent, Mike burned only enough electricity to run his coffee pot and radio. His Sun Bulbs did the rest.

The frame of a 1972 Ducati 750 GT rested on a motorcycle rack, its engine beginning to take shape atop his workbench. It was not so much a restoration as a re-invention. He showed me some of the modifications he had made and talked about those yet to come.

Mike was proud of his work and always eager to talk about it. But sooner or later, as it always does, the discussion turned to old times—the glory days when drugs, money, and adrenaline fueled our lives. Though I have known Mike for over forty years, there was still a lot I didn't know about the early days. I urged him to start at the beginning, his first encounter with the demon weed.

MIKE HALLIDAY

> Okay, it was in the summer of 1967. My son was one year old at the time. I'd been working road construction on the new freeway between El Paso and Las Cruces. I was on the crew of a giant rock crusher—a huge thing that chewed up boulders and spit out gravel. It managed to kill about one guy a year. The centrifugal force and kinetic energy happening there was some serious shit. You couldn't just turn it on and off. If it got you, you were dead.

Anyway, I was back in town on one of my days off and four of us were driving out Montana Street with a couple of six packs. We pulled off on one of the dirt roads—there used to be so many of them out there you could go for days into the desert, then find a completely different road to bring you back.

So my friend Oscar pulls out a joint. Now I had grown up with the understanding that pot was smoked by Mexican gangs right before a street fight so they wouldn't feel the pain of getting beat by chains and steel pipes and stuff. I knew what it was, but I had never tried it or been around it so I watched the first guy take a hit, then the next guy, then Oscar. He handed it to me. Well, I'm no genius, but I knew how to smoke—that was one of my skills. So I took a big hit. And that was probably the most life-changing thing that ever happened to me. I really believe it saved my life.

I was a horrible person. I was a bad drunk, okay? I was eighteen, nineteen years old, and I was an alcoholic. I used to drink quarts of beer just to get the taste in my mouth so I could get on with some serious drinking. And fighting? That's why my hands are all bent to hell. I would be in a bar and see two guys facing off—I had no knowledge of either one of them or what the fight was about. But I'd walk up and announce that I could kick both their asses—that's how stupid I was.

But as soon as I smoked that first joint, I realized I'd found what I was looking for, what I needed in life. And I never even knew I needed it! I was completely flabbergasted by the effect it had on me. I didn't want to fight anybody—didn't need to prove anything to anybody. It was so clear how stupid that was, I was almost embarrassed about it. I knew after that first joint that this was something I didn't want to run out of.

Of course, I worked in New Mexico at the time and I didn't have access to it that much, but when I got back to

El Paso and started smoking more and more, I'd go over to Juarez by myself at night. I'd just drive to the bridge, walk over, and ask a cabbie for some pot. Then I'd put a few joints in my pocket and walk back across the bridge.

Usually I'd wait until I saw a little crowd, like four or five guys that were partying. I'd just kind of get in with them and act like I belonged, and the next thing you know, the inspectors were waving us through. They weren't really looking for pot in those days—they were more worried about people sneaking into the country and illegally mowing your lawn.

HIGHER EDUCATION

Just a few miles west of downtown El Paso, hard by the Rio Grande, stood the University of Texas at El Paso—a little school that did all it could to be taken seriously. UTEP was a stepchild, franchised in the mid-sixties by the mega-rich University of Texas system. Though it tried with all its might to attain the lofty status of its namesake, its only claim to fame so far had been the 1966 NCAA National Basketball Championship, for which the school would receive far more derision than acclaim.

Texas Western College, as it was known in 1966, had won the title starting five black players versus an all-white University of Kentucky team coached by the legendary Adolph Rupp. It was an historic event that galvanized a city and forever altered college basketball. But poor little UTEP couldn't win for losing. They were pilloried by the national press for renting their players, some of whom they labeled as felons and none of whom, they noted, had ever seen the inside of a classroom.

It wasn't true, of course. Several members of the team would settle in El Paso and be embraced by the community. All of them would graduate. None of them had ever been to prison. But as Coach Don Haskins would sadly reflect, "If I had known what the reaction was going to be, I'd just as soon have finished second."

UTEP was mostly a commuter school, though a surprising number of out-of-town students were beginning to enroll. There were only two reasons to go there: the tuition was low and the standards of admission even lower. If you could spell SAT, you were UTEP material, and if you were good for the tuition, they'd probably spot you the S and the T. It was a fledgling university in a remote outpost just west of the middle of nowhere. Everyone with a high-school diploma was gratefully accepted, Jack Stricklin included.

In the '60s, all males were required to register for the draft immediately following their eighteenth birthday. A college deferment was the preferred antidote to the national smash-and-grab that was wasting the better part of a generation in Vietnam. Colleges like UTEP were brimming with students like Jack Stricklin, seeking only shelter from the draft and a good party.

While just about every college experience is punctuated by distraction, higher education in El Paso included the gaudy temptation of Cd. Juarez. It was lost on no one that activities deemed illegal on one side of the border could be made legal simply by crossing a bridge. You could drive your car across and leave a few pesos for a local street gang to watch it, or you could park on the U.S. side and walk over. Either way, you immediately found yourself on The Strip, a half-mile midway of cheap trinkets and bawdy seduction, pulsing to the music of sin and the aroma of tacos al carbon.

Street vendors hawked their wares. Urchins ran to stopped cars to clean their windows with dirty rags. Pimps roamed the brightly lit sidewalks offering all manner of sexual congress with their virgin sisters. Criers stood in the doorways, urging you to step inside and sample the prohibited pleasures. It was the improbable harmony of mariachi and rock 'n roll. And it was irresistible.

At legendary bars like Fred's and the Kentucky Club, fifty cents would get you a mixed drink, thirty-five cents a draft beer. Food was plentiful, cheap, and tasty. And temptation resided on every block. Friday night was boys' night, as the bars and strip joints pulsed to the rhythm of raging hormones. Saturday was date night when the more sophisticated clubs and restaurants played host to awkward young couples desperately seeking to paint a picture of enlightened maturity.

To many of the locals, El Paso and Juarez were not so much viewed as sister cities, but as a single wide-open territory called *la frontera.* Yes, there were bridges and checkpoints. But the inspections were cursory with traffic flowing freely in both directions. And then, of course, there was the river—the mighty Rio Grande, a trickle of mud that did nothing to discourage the free flow of migrants and contraband that had fueled the area economy for more than a hundred years.

Though it had always been available, marijuana was slow to get a foothold among El Paso kids. Like our parents, alcohol was the drug of choice. Underage drinking in Juarez, though certainly not condoned by anyone in authority, was perfectly legal. I may have been a bit on the free-spirited side, but the idea of breaking the law and winding up in prison was something I never would have believed possible. But the war in Vietnam changed all that.

They grew some really good weed over there, a small portion of which managed to find its way back to the States courtesy of the postage-free largesse of Uncle Sam. Vietnamese reefer became a highly coveted commodity and a rare treat for those lucky enough to be on the receiving end. But to the troops on the ground, it was much more than a good high. It was blessed relief from the leech-sucking boredom of continuous crotch-rot, terminal trench foot, and the constant anxiety that any moment could erupt into a lethal firefight.

Vietnam was the last American war fought by conscripts. These were not hardened troops serving in selfless dedication to their country, though many career soldiers fought and died bravely in the effort. Vietnam was a war waged in large part by a diverse collection of unwilling recruits dedicated mainly to their own survival and that of their closest comrades.

Mellow troops might not be happy troops, but as long as the pot flowed freely, the grumbling and dissention were kept to a manageable level. Many of the officers and senior enlisted were willing to look the other way. Some actually encouraged its use. A soldier could function under the influence of pot, some could even excel. A drunken rifleman, however, was good to no one. Of course, Army brass would eventually crack down on cannabis. But that would only lead to a higher incidence of heroin abuse.

The Vietnam War probably did more to kindle the proliferation of marijuana than any other single event. Ironically, marijuana may have played an equally significant role in bringing an end to the war. The first time I ever tasted the divine mellow was with a good buddy who had just returned. "Try it," he told me. "It'll take the edge off." As horrified as I was at the prospects of breaking the law, I was even more terrified of backing down in front of my peers. So I gave it a toke and promptly discovered there was order in the universe after all. It was like a stranger had rented out my brain and rearranged the furniture. All of a sudden, time was no longer bouncing off in random directions, but passing gently in an orderly progression.

"Where has this been? Why have they been telling lies about it? And what the fuck else have they been lying about? You got another one of those?"

To this day, I remember the calm and clarity that came over me in a single deep breath. I can still picture the wallpaper that magically became so interesting. It's an odd thing about potheads. They can hardly remember to zip their fly, but ask them about the first time they ever smoked pot, and you'll get a story told in Technicolor.

Jack Stricklin

The first time I ever smoked pot I was at Doug Holt's house in the Upper Valley—down in his basement. I was dating Ruona. Doug was there with his date, and there were two other couples.

Doug had gotten hold of some pot, but we didn't know how to roll it. So we just emptied out a couple of cigarettes, packed the pot in there and smoked. We each took a hit, and we all were expecting fireworks to start exploding in our heads.

But nothing happened. So we took another hit and nothing happened. By now we're getting a little upset, so we just start smoking 'em as fast as we can. The next thing you know, one of the guys goes into a literal wide-awake coma. He can't move. And the more he can't move, the harder I laugh. Another guy is about ready to shit his pants, he's laughing so hard. Doug Holt goes upstairs and vomits. And we get out another joint, and we smoke that.

Then Ruona says, "Jack, I want to talk to you." And she takes me outside. I'm standing there looking down at her, and she looks about two feet tall with tiny little feet. I can hardly stop laughing. And she said, "Now, you know that this leads to bigger things."

And in my head, I'm saying, "I certainly hope so."

And she says, "We've tried it, it's over with, we're done. This won't happen again."

Well, I knew the minute it hit me that I was going to do it again. My God—I was high as a Georgia pine, totally tuned in to everything around me, and I wasn't going to feel like road kill in the morning. I was out trying to score the very next day.

I learned pretty fast that I didn't have to finance my own habit. I'd buy three lids and sell two. That turned into a half-pound, a pound—whatever I could get, I'd sell to cover the cost, and I'd smoke the rest. The first kilo I ever bought was with a friend just back from the Army. He and I drove down to the south end of Juarez—way out in the boonies. He drove and we ended up in a bar. I remember he was talking to this guy and he came over and said, "Jack, we need $20 to buy this kilo."

"Well, goodness gracious, we've got $50. Are you kidding? Why don't we buy two?"

So we put it in the trunk of the car and drove to the border. They waved us through and that was our first smuggle. We broke it down and sold it quick—it was really good stuff. When it was gone, I started buying from anybody that had it. It turned out a lot of us were buying from the same people who were buying from us. Everybody knew each other and somebody always had pot to sell.

That's how I met Mike Halliday. He was selling to a girl I knew—she introduced us at a party, and we started doing a little business—nothing much. It was more about staying high than making money. Mike Halliday was one of the guys I did business with. Dave Blott was another one. Mike and Dave didn't really know each other, but when I went away to the Navy, they were the guys I counted on to keep me supplied.

CONNECTIONS

In a lot of ways, pot is like Mary Kay Cosmetics. Try it once and you see yourself in a whole new way. Before you know it, you're dealing to all your friends so they can support your $10-a-day lipstick and blush habit.

The only difference is you'll never see a pothead in a pink Cadillac. But at the grass roots, marijuana is all about network marketing. Today's buyer is tomorrow's seller. And everyone shares the high.

In 1969, Mike Halliday was casting weed upon his friends in the handy take-home size. That's what brought him to the little hippie commune on Doniphan Drive in El Paso's Upper Valley. It was a small connection, but it was his first. He scored less than a pound, but before the day was over, Mike would experience the bliss of homemade granola, listen to a little Bob Dylan, and witness a spectacular high-desert sunset.

In the time it took to break in a new pair of Levi's, Mike Halliday became a tie-dyed hippie. He grew a ponytail and converted his VW bus into a slick camper with a cleverly concealed "hide" to preserve his stash. A few performance-enhancing modifications of his own design were added, of course. But the crowning glory was the large peace symbol that replaced the VW logo on the front of the bus. *Make Love, Not War* may have been the statement he was trying to make, but he couldn't have screamed *ARREST MY ASS!* any louder with a billboard and a bullhorn.

Mike Halliday

My wife Karen turned into Earth Mother and I was a hippie with a job—which made me kind of a part-time hippie. But I was lucky enough to get on at Phelps Dodge—the copper refinery down on Trowbridge Street. It was hard work, but the pay was really good. It turned out I was the very first gringo in eight years that lasted more than sixty days. The only gringos there at the time were the machinists and the foremen and office guys.

I worked down the line from the shears, where the copper was cut into pieces weighing about seventy-five pounds each. Part of my job was to stack 'em up for shipping. The thing is, this copper would have growths on it kind of like warts. By the time you stacked 'em about three feet high, they would be leaning every which way, looking like they were going to fall over. So every time I saw a big wart, I'd flip the sheet and turn it so it would come down on the other side—the smooth side. My stacks would always come out nice and straight.

The shipping department thought I was a genius. They wanted me to show the other guys how to do it that way, but I think they had me confused with somebody who wanted to experience an industrial accident. These guys had been working there for fifteen years—they weren't gonna like some gringo kid showing them a better way. I kept my mouth shut. Turned out to be a good decision too, because a lot of the Mexicans ended up liking me.

I had a Volkswagen van I converted to a camper. I always smoked a joint on the way to work. I wore tinted safety glasses inside Phelps Dodge, so you couldn't see my eyes. I could get high, go stack my copper or whatever job they gave me, and no one would ever know. At noon, I'd go out by the smokestack and smoke another joint by myself.

I thought I was pretty cool about it, but it turns out the Mexicans all knew I was getting high. They started asking me if I wanted to smoke some of their pot.

"Okay—whatever. Pot's pot." But the first joint—hell, the first hit was a different story. That was some primo shit—the best pot I had ever smoked and probably my first taste of really good Mexican. It made the stuff I'd been getting from the hippies look like alfalfa.

I went drinking all the time with these guys from Phelps Dodge—they hung out in a little bar on Alameda Street. In those days you could go in there and buy a Prince Albert can of pretty good pot for $10. Some of the guys just let you reach in the bag—as much as your hand would hold, that was $5.

They hooked me up pretty good—a kilo or two at a time. So I got to where I started selling more and more—to the hippies, friends and neighbors, and a few other guys. And they had some friends who had some friends…you know how it was. If you had pot, you had friends. I was getting a lot of friends.

That was about the time I met Jack Stricklin. It was at a party thrown by an old girlfriend of his—she introduced us and we hit it off right away. Jack was a college guy, but he wasn't a douche bag. We started doing a little business, nothing much—nickel and dime shit. Jack got to be one of my regular customers. He was always trying to hook me up with a friend of his named Dave Blott. Dave was another guy he bought from. Every time I got with Jack, he was always trying to get us together.

Dave Blott was a friend of Jack Stricklin—one of the neighborhood guys who would stop by our house from time to time. I didn't really know Dave. The five or six year difference in our ages seemed eternal, and neither of us had much interest in closing the gap. Dave graduated from the neighborhood high school, served a hitch in the Navy, and came home to find whatever work he could as an electrician.

The Navy had introduced Dave Blott to the bliss of cannabis. He found no shortage of ways to maintain a steady supply once he got out. He was, after all, living in El Paso. As a friend of Jack Stricklin, it was only natural that they would do business, sharing small loads of a kilo or two and breaking them down at $10 an ounce. Like Jack, Dave began to see the possibilities of scaling up. But Jack was going away to serve his own hitch in the Navy. He tried in vain to put Dave Blott together with Mike Halliday. But as good as he was at making connections, Jack Stricklin had thus far failed to link his two most reliable sources of supply.

MIKE HALLIDAY

At the time, I was living in the alley on Hastings Street. It was actually a house that was in the alley. And right across the alley was another little house. Anyway, this place had a glass-enclosed porch that was full of mismatched stuff. It was too cold to sleep there in the winter and too hot in the summer. We lived there probably two and a half years. The only time I slept in that little room was on that night. My son Mikey had an earache so I put him in bed with Karen. That's why I was on the porch.

It's about ten or eleven o'clock. I hear a car drive up and park in the alley, and I think, "Oh shit, is somebody here to see us?"

I look outside. It's the guy who lives across the alley and another guy. They get out and open the trunk and start pulling out duffel bags and hauling them inside. I'm like, "Holy shit!" It didn't take a genius to figure that one out, right? It was probably more pot in one place than I'd ever seen.

So the next afternoon, I'm waiting for my neighbor when he pulls up around 4:30. He gets out of the car, and I say, "Hey, I live across the alley, I'm Mike."

"Yeah, I know who you are," he says.

"Well," I say, "I just want to talk to you about something."

"What's that?"

"I happened to be on the porch last night when you guys pulled up." He gets this look on his face like he doesn't know whether to shit or go blind. So I say, "Hey, I just want to buy something, man."

That turned out to be Dave Blott. It kind of shows you what a small town El Paso was back then. Here's this guy Jack was always trying to put me together with, and there he was living right across the alley about twenty feet away.

ANCHORS & CHAINS

The issues Jack Stricklin would have with authority were a minor annoyance compared to the issues authority would have with Jack Stricklin. With pot consuming more and more of his time and Jack consuming more and more pot, school ranked somewhere below *wash the car* on his list of priorities. Academic probation was followed smartly by double academic probation, which preceded academic suspension.

After about a year and a half of college, Jack had finally exhausted his final reprieve. He was reclassified 1-A, declared fit for service and about to receive his greetings from the local draft board. Few escaped military induction in the late '60s.

To Jack, joining the Navy seemed the least objectionable alternative to the rifle and rucksack clusterfuck of Vietnam. The Navy, of course, was in Vietnam up to its waterline, but they mostly slept in soft beds and ate hot chow. The only downside to enlistment was a four-year hitch versus the two years Jack would have owed had the draft come calling. The Navy attracted more than its share of college boys willing to serve, but unwilling to be sacrificed. *Be All You Can Be* resonated with far more appeal than *Join the Army and Die.* Unfortunately for the Navy, education and blind obedience were largely incompatible qualities among recruits of the day. But this was the era of the body count and Jack Stricklin's body would count just fine on the deck of a ship headed, of course, to Vietnam.

Jack would handle the Navy like he handled everything else—

he would make the best of it. His father had served, and he too would do his duty. But he did it on his own terms, which actually meant doing as little of his duty as was humanly possible.

Jack had been assigned to the USS Wichita, the lead ship of the Wichita class replenishment oilers. Having undergone refitting at the Boston Naval Shipyard, the ship made its way to Long Beach where he joined the crew. In a few months they would be refueling ships operating on Yankee Station in the South China Sea.

Jack Stricklin found his groove in the spit-and-polish Navy thanks to the one ability he actually mastered in high school— typing. If you're going to fight a war, the typewriter may not be the sexiest weapon in the arsenal, but it could be the most powerful. Armed with little but a lightweight bond and a single sheet of carbon paper, Typist Mate Jack Stricklin could inflict more damage than a company of Rangers. Here is where the true power lies. Single-spaced, in triplicate.

It was a job he could do in a coma. Jack spent most of his time staying high, and the rest making sure every shipmate who cared to join him was well-supplied. Even then, Jack knew he didn't want to sell joints or grams. The reward hardly justified the risk. So he organized a network of distributors to sell his pot from stem to stern, making sure there was ample margin for everyone. It was his first real distribution network and it seemed to be working just fine.

With Mike Halliday and Dave Blott keeping him supplied, Jack was probably making as much money every month as most of the officers in his chain of command. He was definitely having more fun as he counted off his days on an advent calendar stocked with tightly rolled joints. It took Jack Stricklin no time at all to figure out the Navy and how best to endure his hitch. Now it was just a matter of doing the time.

JACK STRICKLIN

Mike Halliday and Dave Blott were my suppliers. One or the other usually had pot. At first, they'd send me a little for my own personal use. Then everybody started coming to me, so I'd get more and more.

Mike was a total genius when it came to packaging pot. He'd seal it up in coffee cans, cereal boxes, cookie tins—all the things you'd send a guy in the service. The pot was always manicured and packaged like it just came off the shelf. I was getting the whole ship high.

One of the guys on the ship—a black guy—he was a regular buyer—a distributor. He was a good guy. I'd even front him the pot sometimes. He always paid. Well, one day this guy gets in a fight with another guy—I mean, he beat nine shades of shit out of him. And the guy that took the beating got even by ratting him out.

So when the Shore Patrol shows up to arrest my guy, they find a list of names that he carried in his pocket. My name was at the top. Well, they came down on me even harder than they came down on him. They offered me everything but a commission if I would name names. But that wasn't going to happen, so I was court martialed and convicted—my first pot bust. It was an eye-opener.

The lesson I learned was that it's not always your own fuckup that gets you. You can be as careful as you want, but if you don't surround yourself with people who are smart and loyal, you're not going to survive. What kind of fucking pot dealer walks around with the name of his supplier written down in his pocket?

I never for one minute thought I was going to quit dealing. But I thought a lot about how to do it better. And I had a lot of time to think. I was sitting in the Long Beach brig when the ship deployed to Vietnam. I rode the chain from there to San Diego, then to Portsmouth, New Hampshire and the Naval and Marine Corps prison.

The prison in Portsmouth was a fucking dungeon. There were some bad motherfuckers inside, maximum-security, maybe the scariest prison I've ever been in. You didn't have to wonder who was a killer—they all were. But in a funny way that worked out for me, because I knew if I could survive there, I could survive anywhere. The prospect of doing time never scared me after that.

A lot of people might have been discouraged to find themselves in a maximum-security military prison. The food was lousy, beds hard, inmates largely homicidal. There was not a lot of fun to be had. But Jack possessed several unusual qualities that would enable him to adapt. One, he was a world-class sleeper. He could take a nap on the business end of a jackhammer. Doing time was a whole lot easier when you were unconscious. Two, he had a knack for making friends to help him pass the time. And three, he could score pot in a convent.

"Dear Mike," he wrote. "It really sucks in here. It sure would be nice if you could do something for my smile…"

Mike Halliday knew, of course, that all mail in and out of prison was carefully screened. He took it as a personal challenge, meticulously manicuring the finest Mexican pot and packing it perfectly into an emptied tube of Crest toothpaste. He added small nails to achieve the exact weight then resealed the tube in its original box. It was as pristine as the day it left the line. He tossed in a toothbrush for good measure and included a short note.

Dear Jack, Sorry I can't help you out, bro. I'm afraid this is all I can do for your smile.

FITS & STARTS

Mike Halliday

I had this guy in Cleveland—a black guy I had sold to when he was stationed at Fort Bliss. He called me one day after he got out of the Army and said he wanted about twenty-five pounds, which I ended up getting from Dave Blott. But I couldn't take the time off from work to drive it to him, and he didn't want to come get it.

So the first thing I did was build a bricking machine—my first one. Honestly, it was a piece of shit, but I managed to press the pot into bricks, exactly the size of milk cartons. Then I sealed them with wax—dog proof, right? I packed those milk cartons in an old footlocker and threw some worthless shit on top. Then I went down to the Greyhound station and put it on the bus to Cleveland.

For some reason, the guy in Cleveland never came and got it. I don't know if he thought the load was hot, or if he found Jesus, or if he was just a chickenshit. But he never picked it up. So I went down to the bus station and had it sent back—it was twenty-five pounds of pot. I wasn't about to let Greyhound have it.

By the time I got it back, that footlocker had stickers on it from as far away as Detroit, and it was beat to shit. Greyhound sent that thing everywhere. But nobody ever got a sniff of that pot. I ended up fronting the whole load to a guy I knew in El Paso.

A couple of days later, I opened the morning paper and right there in the Borderland section was a picture of those milk cartons. The caption said, "Police Seize Dog-Proof Pot." It was the first load I ever lost.

Somewhere around that same time, I met these guys from Tennessee. They were just walking around San Jacinto Plaza in downtown El Paso trying to score. So happens one of the guys I worked with at Phelps Dodge, a Mexican dude, he wanted to get a sideline job, so I gave him some of my garbage stuff to sell. And there he was working the Plaza when these guys from Tennessee ran into him. My guy knew he didn't have enough, so he said, "Okay, I'll take you to someone I know." And they all show up in my alley.

Well, I really didn't have much to sell either. Dave had nothing. So I called a friend of mine—The General. The name was kind of a joke because he took ROTC in high school and he was pretty gung-ho about it. I didn't do a lot of business with him. He was kind of a nervous kid, not really cut out to be a drug dealer. But he had a decent connection, which was more than Dave or I had then.

It turns out The General had taken all his pot out to the desert and buried it. So we get in his car with a couple of shovels and head east out past Horizon City and Cattlemen's Steakhouse. We end up about forty miles outside the city limits in the middle of fucking nowhere.

Anyway, we dug up the pot, and I delivered it to the guys from Tennessee—about thirty-five pounds. They probably got a few pounds free because I forgot to bring a scale. But I got a good price and made a nice profit for a couple hours work.

These guys had never seen Mexican pot with the little white seeds before and had no idea what to expect. So we tried it out before they left town. About halfway through the second joint, they were falling all over themselves. They said it was the best pot they had ever smoked. They took my phone number and swore they would stay in touch. But a year later I still hadn't heard a word.

At this point, Mike Halliday was just another hamster on the wheel, spinning in place as he sifted through the moment in search of spare parts he might fashion into something bigger and better. He and Dave Blott were selling all the pot they could get their hands on, but Dave's product was overpriced and the quality inconsistent. Mike could only get a kilo or two at a time from his Phelps Dodge connections, but he sensed they were closer to the source than Dave Blott had ever been. A groundswell of pot smokers was emerging in America. And Mike Halliday knew he was standing on the ground that was swelling.

El Paso has always been a smugglers' paradise, engraved with the colorful legend of a wide-open border town that defined the rules of commerce on its own terms. Smuggling was an important part of the area's economy and largely viewed with a wink and a nod, as everything from human traffic and livestock to cosmetics and cigarettes flowed freely across the invisible boundary. We were a forgotten city, carved from the foothills of the Rocky Mountains and slowed to a crawl by the ceaseless heat of an eternally blazing sun. Not quite Old Mexico, not quite New Mexico, not exactly Texas, but an isolated frontier town with a self-determining soul and an outlaw spirit. Laws were mere suggestions and contraband was just another word for bargain.

Living the better part of your childhood in a border town instills a Latino ethic that defies provenance. The rich and contagious culture became deeply embedded in our lives, heavily accented with the local spice of good friends, fiery food, and a language all its own. But while growing up gringo allowed us to absorb the best of a native heritage, we were spared the worst. The hometown that I knew in the 1970s was a largely integrated city, but not without discrimination. El Paso resided in poverty, controlled by the handful of Anglos who comprised its economic core.

If you were inside the great white bubble, opportunity would present itself. If you were Mexican, you waited at the back of the line. And you didn't concern yourself with impractical laws that attempted to govern an ungovernable frontier. What stereotyping so unfairly sketched as a mañana mentality was simply an acceptance of the fact that when you're powerless to *make* things happen, you have to *let* things happen.

Mike Halliday was certain that good things would happen within the confines of Phelps Dodge. But all he could do was go to work every day, stack his copper, and continue to build trust with *los hermanos*, who were beginning to accept him as "Guero," a light-skinned Mexican. Mike knew he was getting close, just as he knew that he was living in the land of the all-night menudo parlor, where life moved to the rhythm of its own unhurried beat. Gather your family and friends, kill a goat, bury it in the coals, and pop a cool one. We'll laugh, talk, and make music until the sun comes up. Then we'll see what tomorrow brings.

MIKE HALLIDAY

In 1970, I'd been working at Phelps Dodge about a year and a half when I met Panchelli. He was a heroin addict, but a functional heroin addict. And he knew people. We'd been out drinking a few times and we smoked pot together. One day he offered to take me to Juarez, where he knew a guy who would sell us as much as we wanted. And then he would show me where to bring it across.

Just what I was looking for, right? The only problem was I didn't have any money.

What got me started—what really set things in motion was a camping trip I took with my wife Karen up to Wall

Lake in the Gila Wilderness. She was about seven and a half months pregnant at the time, but her doctor said it would be okay. Her father let me take an old school bus he had fixed up for camping.

From the ranger station on the highway, Wall Lake was about eight miles of very rough road. We got there as the sun was going down. Karen was riding in the back and all that bouncing around was not a smart idea. The first thing out of her mouth the next morning was, "I'm going to have the baby!"

So we pack up and head back to the Ranger station. The Ranger's wife talked to Karen and told her husband to get a helicopter there right now. They turned out to be really great people. They took care of my son Michael John while we flew to Silver City in the helicopter.

Well, evidently, a pregnant couple in a helicopter is a pretty big news day in Silver City. We made the front page of the paper—a picture of us landing in the parking lot. Linda Jean Halliday was born on May 21, 1970. She stayed in the hospital for a little over a week.

Now, because Silver City is a big copper city, some of the bosses at Phelps Dodge got the newspaper from up there. I was still a big story when I got back to work. Before I drove back to Silver City to pick up Karen and the baby, the insurance people cut me a check for $700—made out to *me*, not the hospital!

That was the thing that really started everything rolling. That $700 got me my first Mexican load.

We were in my mom's little white Valiant and Panchelli and I are driving along in Mexico with about twenty-five pounds of pot in the trunk. We might have been thinking about how we were going to spend the money—we were definitely not thinking about the speed limit. Not very smart—Mexican cops make a living on traffic tickets.

So this guy pulls us over for speeding and starts talking about going to see the judge. Panchelli got out to talk to him while I freaked out. I knew the guy would take a payoff, but I had spent every last dime on the weed, and Panchelli was a junkie—he never had any money. So he was talking to the cop and pointing to me in the car, and the whole time the cop kept nodding his head.

When Panchelli came back to the car, he told me to take off my watch but act like I didn't want to give it up. So I kept shaking my head *no* while I handed to him. That watch probably cost about ten bucks new—it was junk. But that piece-of-shit watch saved our ass that day. We gave it to the cop like it was some kind of solid gold Rolex. He put it in his pocket and let us go. I just hoped we'd get across the river before it stopped running.

Panchelli had me drive to a place he knew down past Tornillo. He told me to carry the load across the river, and he'd drive back over the bridge and meet me on the other side of the levee, where I'd be hiding with the pot.

It was broad daylight, man, but the area was totally deserted. You could see a long way in any direction. I could have stopped and smoked a joint in the middle of the river. I walked across, climbed to the other side of the levee and found a nice little place to stash the weed. After about thirty minutes, here comes Panchelli in the Valiant and away we go.

After a couple of those kinds of deals, I started to get pretty tight with Panchelli's connection. That was Hector—Hector was the guy. He was connected to Sinaloa—the big fields, the best pot. The problem was, you could only throw so many bags over your back and carry it across like that. What we needed was a four-wheel drive.

HOMECOMING
JACK STRICKLIN
1970

Bottom to top: Jack Stricklin, Mike and Karen Halliday, Dave and Joyce Blott, ca. 1970

After four months and twenty-six days in maximum security, the Navy drove me to the middle of downtown Boston and let me out. Under their own guidelines, they couldn't give me a dishonorable discharge so I got a BCD (bad conduct discharge). I honestly didn't care. I was out—that was all that mattered.

My family had a cabin in Durango, Colorado—that's where I went first. I didn't have a car. I had sold my Plymouth when I went in the Navy. My goal at the time was to earn $10,000. I don't know why I picked that amount or what I would do if I ever earned that much. But that's what I wanted to do. And I was headed to El Paso to hook up with Mike and Dave.

My parents had no idea how I'd finished out my time in the Navy. My sister Bonnie knew. I'd send her letters and she'd send them to a friend of mine on the ship, and he'd send them to my folks.

I only stayed a couple of days in Durango. About the time I was thinking of leaving, Dad says, "Jack, what are you going to do now?"

"Well, I'm going to El Paso, earn a little money and see some friends."

"What are you going to be driving?"

"I don't know, I'll probably buy some old jalopy when I get there."

"Well, I'll tell you what, Jack. We're going to shut down the cabin for the winter anyway. Why don't you take the Scout and drive it 'til you find something else. You can bring it back in the spring."

"Welcome to Texas," read the sign by the side of the road. Within range of El Paso at last, Jack Stricklin drummed the wheel to the rhythm of the radio as the four-wheel drive International Scout carried him home. Just to the north, La Tuna Federal Correctional Institute crowned a gradual rise. It was a quiet presence to all but the unfortunate souls housed within.

With the Franklin Mountains just ahead, Jack looked out over Mexico to the south, where primitive huts randomly dotted the small mesa that rose from the trickle of the Rio Grande. Tendrils of wood smoke drifted from makeshift chimneys, merging with the poisonous reek from the towering smokestack of El Paso's ASARCO lead smelter. As if total poverty was not enough, the riverside colonia endured an air quality that condemned its children to the lethal fate of lead poisoning.

Just past ASARCO and the University, Interstate 10 came to a slingshot curve, skirting the southern tip of Mount Franklin and heading east. The edge of downtown El Paso and its sleepy railroad yard, once so important to the economy, flew by in a blink. Jack Stricklin was back on the border, where the only law that really mattered was: *Don't get caught.*

Jack Stricklin never thought of himself as a criminal. He believed in justice and more than a few of the *Thou Shalt Not's*. But he didn't believe in all of them. As far as he was concerned, a crime without a victim was an opportunity. Enforcing the prohibition of marijuana made no more sense than enforcing the prohibition against alcohol. It was a mistake in the 1930s, it is a mistake now. And just like the bootleggers before him, it was a mistake Jack Stricklin fully intended to exploit.

JACK STRICKLIN

> When I pulled into the alley where Mike Halliday lived, the last person I expected to see was Dave Blott. I honked the horn and started to get out, and here came Mike out of one house and Dave out the other one. I'd been trying to get these two assholes together the whole time I was in the Navy, and here they were living twenty feet away from each other.
>
> When I got out to say hello, they walked right past me. They were staring at that four-wheel drive Scout like it was a carne asada. The first thing either one of them said to me was, "Jack, we need to borrow your truck."

MIKE HALLIDAY

> When Jack shows up in our alley in that Scout, Dave and I come out and walk right past him. Jack's like, "I'm home!" And we're thinking, *Oh, thank you God—this is perfect*!
>
> We got him to take us for a ride down to the place where we wanted to bring a load across. Once you got past Fabens, the river is bone dry—the farmers have taken all the water. You could dribble a basketball across. So you drive through the riverbed, then you've got the levee on the other side, and there's a big ditch that's even steeper

than the riverbank itself. So we walked across and showed Jack what we had in mind and he said, "Oh, hell yeah." We locked the hubs into four-wheel drive and drove across and back—easy. That little Scout ate it up.

So that night we did our first load. Jack couldn't go— we didn't have room for three guys and all the pot, so he stayed home.

Jack Stricklin

The night Mike and Dave took the Scout was probably the longest night of my life. I was so nervous I thought I was going to throw up. That might have been the first time I ever worried about anything. I wasn't worried when the Navy sent me to Portsmouth. I never worried about school—nothing. But I let two idiots go out in my father's Scout to bring a load of pot across the river, and I couldn't stop thinking about how many ways they could fuck it up.

I paced the floor, chainsmoked joints, and cussed myself for being such a dumbass. I actually made a vow that night that I would never feel that way again. The next time anybody brought a load of pot across the river, I was going to be there to make damn sure we did it right.

Mike Halliday

That was the night I discovered how different everything looks in the dark. Your whole world comes down to what's right in front of your face. You have no idea what's out there. It was just Dave and me. We didn't have any radios, no spotters—just two clueless guys driving around in the dark with 250 pounds of pot.

The first place we pulled in along the river was the wrong place—it was too muddy. We didn't have our headlights on and we couldn't see shit. And when we got to the river there was nowhere to cross so we had to backtrack. The whole time we just knew the Border Patrol was going to pop up out of the bushes. We were sure the cicadas were sending some kind of secret fed signal. It was like every cell in my brain was sending a different message. And time just stopped. When we finally got to a dry spot in the river, I was ready to just floor the motherfucker and keep on going.

We somehow managed to keep it together. "Bump, bump, bump," down the bank and across the riverbed. "Bump, bump, bump"—up the bank, over the levee and gone.

Dave and I couldn't stop laughing. It worked perfect. It was the highest of highs I had ever experienced in my life. It was only 250 pounds or so, but it was our first real smuggle. We couldn't get over ourselves.

THE GRANDMOTHER
OF ALL CONNECTIONS

Mike Halliday

That first smuggle with Jack's Scout—that got things moving pretty fast. But now we were looking for buyers. One day Dave Blott came by and said, "I got these guys, they're sitting in a motel, and they want some pot. You want to go with me to meet with them?"

So I went with him. As soon as I came through the door, this guy hollers, "Mike!" And here were these Tennessee people back in town, and they had somehow run into Dave. Once again, fate played a huge part in all this.

I knew Jack got arrested in the Navy because some dumbass was walking around with his phone number in his pocket, so I always gave my phone number out in code. It was a simple one—probably wouldn't fool anybody for long. Of course, these guys forgot the key to break the code. They said they'd been trying to find me ever since we did that first deal in the desert.

The guys were from Tennessee—Tommy Pitts and John Wheeler. They turned out to be a really good connection in the early time. They put together some decent buyers of their own and took a lot of weight. If I remember right, I think we started with around 200 pounds. After that, they wanted more and more. Dave could never keep up with anything like that—the suppliers he had were spotty. So Jack and I took 'em on, and Dave was more or less a partner. That's when things started getting serious—that's when we got with Hector and really started to roll.

Hector Ruiz Gonzales, aka El Arabe, was a well-connected Mexican whose stock in trade was heroin and opium. He was astute enough to recognize a growth industry when he saw one. As the pot phenomenon began to gain momentum, Hector was front and center. And by his side was Mike Halliday, whom he had met through Panchelli and nurtured from one small deal to the next.

Though no one realized it at the time, Mike had landed a twenty-four karat connection. From stubborn persistence and a snarl of disparate parts, he untangled his way to numero uno—the man who controlled the biggest fields in Northern Mexico. Just like Panchelli and the boys at Phelps Dodge, Hector took an immediate liking to Mike. They were similar in age and temperament, firmly attached to the values of machismo, and united in their desire to plumb the border and open the spigots wide. To Hector, Mike was still a small buyer with the potential to grow. To Mike, Hector was the mother lode.

In this case, the mother lode would actually turn out to be Hector's grandmother. Her name was Ignacia Jasso Gonzalez, but she was better known as La Nacha.

La Nacha was a one-woman cartel before the cartels ever rose to prominence. And she was the absolute monarch of Northern Mexico's illicit drug trade. In fact, La Nacha ruled the wide-open badlands for more than a half-century. To this day, her name is uttered in hushed tones of respect along Mexico's northern border.

La Nacha was likely to have been born sometime in the early

1890's, which would make her around seventy-eight when Mike Halliday entered the picture in the early '70s. She had ascended the ranks through marriage to a smuggler called El Pablote, her first boss, her mentor, and a man who would himself become a drug kingpin in Mexico. Together, they would remove the Chinese opium dealers who held a tight rein on the Mexican drug trade. The Mexicans hated the Chinese drug dealers. Few took notice and even fewer took exception when La Nacha and El Pablito eliminated them with extreme prejudice.

But payback's a bitch. After the untimely assassination of El Pablote in 1927 or so, La Nacha was left to run things on her own. She discovered an aptitude for the business and grew it impressively, rising above the law. Her activities were hardly a secret, but widespread "donations" kept her safely outside the extremely short reach of Mexican law enforcement. She applied la mordida (the bite) with a liberal hand.

How much money she made was anybody's guess. In 1973, the *El Paso Herald Post* reported that La Nacha had amassed close to $4.5 million in safe deposit boxes throughout Cd. Juarez. Yet she refused to budge from Bellavista, the working-class Juarez neighborhood where she lived most of her adult life.

By many reports, La Nacha ruled with a benevolent hand, funding programs for hungry children and unwed mothers. Who knows? But her power was absolute as she reigned supreme over the shooting gallery near downtown Juarez, where opiates were dispensed to anyone with the price of a fix.

MIKE HALLIDAY

> La Nacha was never called La Nacha in Mexico. She was La Senora. She dealt heroin out of a little house in a row of houses in a neighborhood. The house next door was Hector's office. Hector ran the shooting gallery for his grandmother. It had a screen door. There would be a guy who just stood there. His job was to let you in. Once you

got inside, there was an old car seat and a little table with a bottle of water and a bunch of needles. Hygiene was non-existent.

Another guy would sit at the little table with a moneybag and three different pouches. He had a gun next to him. They sold it three different ways—$40 for a gram, $10 for a hit, or $5 for the really shitty stuff.

After being a lookout for years, then working the door for years, this guy finally gets the chance to sell the actual heroin. You know how much he gets paid for selling heroin? Nothing—not a dime. What he gets is the chance to rip people off—especially the gringos. They'd ask for $10 worth, he'd give them $5 and they wouldn't know the difference. The Mexican junkies and most of the real hardcore junkies, they could tell. But the guy could make a lot of money ripping people off at $5 a whack, because it was a 24/7 business.

And every Monday without fail—rain, shine—there was a guy who would sit in a lawn chair out at the corner and wear a big straw hat. He had a spiral notebook and a bag of money. If you were a Mexican cop, all you had to do was drive by, sign your name, put down your badge number. That's it, you're $10 richer.

So when the Federales came to town a couple of times a year, the local cops would be sure and tell La Nacha in advance. She'd shut down and go spend a few days at the ranch. That woman was better protected than the President of Mexico. She had so much money you wondered why she lived where she did. But she owned four blocks in every direction from her house. And along with all the houses, she owned the people. So if anybody wanted to get to her, they had to go through four square blocks of Mexicans. And they all had guns.

The early success enjoyed by Mike and Jack was not so much a case of outsmarting the authorities as an absence of any authorities to outsmart. In 1968, under Lyndon Johnson, the Bureau of Narcotics, administered by the Treasury Department, was combined with the Bureau of Drug Abuse Control (BDAC), which operated as part of the Department of Health, Education, and Welfare. The newly formed Bureau of Narcotics and Dangerous Drugs (BNDD) was the latest in an alphabet soup of drug enforcement agencies.

Immortalized in the Academy-Award winning movie, "The French Connection," the BNDD made its bones in the international heroin trade. Marijuana had not yet gotten their attention. What little resistance Mike and Jack encountered came in the form of the Border Patrol, an overworked, understaffed agency with an impossible job and inadequate funding. Three thousand miles of border divided by several hundred agents equals token resistance. Their focus was on illegal aliens. If they happened to stumble on a drug crossing, so much the better. But it wasn't high on their list of priorities.

Hector kept the loads coming. The Tennessee connection began to absorb up to 1,000 pounds at a time. Significant buyers in Colorado and Florida were coming into play. The loads grew quickly as Jack Stricklin focused on the distribution side while Mike Halliday spent his time in Mexico, where he was beginning to discover that the business of pot adhered to an entirely different code of conduct.

MIKE HALLIDAY

It was sometime in the early '70s. Mexico had decided that the United States had something wrong with their horses—some kind of equestrian flu. I think they called it Operation Grand Vision. They wanted to make sure no American horses were being smuggled into Mexico.

So the local army decided okay, our job is to go and

make sure nobody crosses the border. Well, it took them zero minutes to find out where the best smuggling routes were. There were places that were just so heavily used for smuggling, they might as well have had traffic lights. The only ones that didn't know about 'em were our own feds. So the Mexican Army sets up camp at the spot we liked to use—right there at the bottom of the levee.

We found out about it pretty fast. Hector, Panchelli, and myself—we go down there in the middle of the day and find the head guy. We told him we were going to be coming through there at night with some TVs from Mexico. We tell them, "We're gonna be driving this vehicle across right here, and it's gonna be about ten tonight." Of course by now a couple hundred dollars have changed hands, so the guy said, "No problemo. You bring all the TVs you want. We're ready for you at ten."

That night, I drove the Scout. By now we had bought one of our own. Dave and Jack were up on the highway. We had our radios and scanners going, everything looked okay. I turned off the lights because it was a fairly full moon. I came down the levee and headed into the river.

The minute I got down the bank and into the riverbed, I swear I could hear the firing pin hit the first bullet. All of a sudden—*Bam, bam*. Holy shit they're shooting at me!

It's really kind of funny. The first thing you do when you're getting shot at from behind is crinkle up your neck. Like somehow, that's gonna stop a bullet. In real life, what really saves you is when you got 600 pounds of pot behind you. It takes a pretty high-powered round to get through that.

Well, I'm coming up the other bank, and then I had to get up on the levee where I'd be perfectly silhouetted. It was almost like shooting ducks in the carnival. *Bam, bam, bam*! Jack is on the fucking radio, "Hey, Dave, are you shooting your gun?"

And I'm screaming "Is it clear? Is it clear? Get me the fuck out of here!"

I mean we got out of there in a hurry. I figured the gas tank would explode at any moment. I was driving like a maniac. Somehow I got out of there without getting killed.

When we got back to my house—we were living down the Valley at that time, pretty close to the river—we looked over that Scout, there was not one fucking bullet hole to be found anywhere! That's impossible—that Scout had to be shot to hell. But we couldn't find one bullet hole.

The next day we went back to the river and asked the commander, "What the hell was that about?"

Those cocksuckers were still drunk. They must have spent every dime we paid them on tequila and beer. "Oh, amigo, we want to make it look good—yes? I tell the guys, when the gringos come, you shoot over the head—*Bam, bam, bam, bam.* Good one, huh?"

TOKEN RESISTANCE

If there's one image that perfectly captures the futility of America's long and hopeless War on Drugs, it might be the 1971 photograph of a bizarre Oval Office summit between President Richard Nixon, perfectly polished and typically uneasy, posing side-by-side with his first volunteer in the newly declared war, G-Man-wannabe Elvis Presley.

Toned down for the occasion in basic black and tastefully accessorized with a crime-fighting cape and a gold buckle the size of a Krispy Kreme, the aging Elvis stood ready to take arms against the illicit trade, asking only for a badge (preferably gold) and a license to kill. The clinically paranoid Nixon was convinced the spread of marijuana was a dark conspiracy brought to bear by commie potheads. As he stated on a White House tape, "...that's why the Communists and the left-wingers are pushing the stuff. They're trying to destroy us from within."

America's misunderstanding of marijuana is largely the result of a long history of ignorance and racism. Prior to the 1930s, pot was legal and untaxed. But a man named Harry Anslinger changed all that.

In 1929, J. Edgar Hoover chose Anslinger to head up the Department of Prohibition. Following the repeal of the alcohol ban in 1933, however, there was no Department left to run. So Harry Anslinger was given the top spot at the Federal Bureau of Narcotics. Anslinger, who would publicly state that marijuana was no big deal, promptly changed his tune. He knew that heroin and cocaine enforcement would not be enough to sustain an entire department, so he took on cannabis.

Harry Anslinger went on to run the Federal Narcotics Bureau until 1962. During his long tenure, he played a significant role in the Marijuana Tax Act of 1937, outlawing possession and sale. He spearheaded the American premiere of "Reefer Madness," a propaganda film so heavy-handed it has become the must-see cult classic of stoners everywhere. Anslinger vilified cannabis at every opportunity, applying an undercoat of racism that slanted enforcement heavily toward Mexicans and African-Americans. It was Anslinger himself who was credited with the popularization of the word *marijuana* to more heavily associate it with Mexicans. And he once proclaimed, "Reefer makes darkies think they're as good as white men."

It wasn't until marijuana found its way to the middle-class that government began to take notice. In 1970, Congress passed the Comprehensive Drug Abuse and Control Act, which temporarily placed pot in the pantheon of dangerous narcotics, Schedule One, residing at the right hand of heroin.

In 1971, Nixon created a special Presidential Commission to examine the "marijuana problem" and issue recommendations. He appointed Pennsylvania Governor and former hardline prosecutor Richard Shafer to head the commission. Shafer had been a law-and-order governor. The administration felt he could be relied on to get tough on weed. Shafer himself even admitted to a pre-conceived anti-pot bias.

In the course of their due diligence, the commission heard testimony from police, judges, doctors, politicians, students, lawyers, and others. They conducted surveys and research, even traveled abroad to learn how other countries dealt with the issue. By all reports it was a thorough job.

Despite unrelenting pressure from the White House, the Shafer Commission would ultimately conclude that marijuana caused "no significant physical, chemical, or mental abnormalities," and that "Most users demonstrate an average or above-average degree of social functioning, academic achievement, and job performance." They concluded that marijuana use did not lead to violent behavior nor was it a gateway to heroin or other drugs.

Nixon and Elvis were not amused. The administration, in fact, simply ignored the report and turned up the heat. Marijuana-related arrests spiked by over 130,000 between 1972 and 1973, totaling some 420,000. The large importers continued to operate with impunity as law enforcement aggressively chased street dealers and users, parading them before the media like kingpins. Make no mistake, the early days of Nixon's war on drugs was a war on pot. And to further complicate his spectacularly failing presidency, pot was winning.

Mike Halliday

One night Jack and I were down on the river checking out a new place we were thinking of using. It was pretty late, when we got in the car to head back. As soon as we hit the freeway, we got pulled over by the Border Patrol.

It was back in the hippie days and I still had a ponytail. So Jack got out of the driver side and went back to talk to the Border Patrol agent. The guy started looking around with his flashlight. When he saw the ponytail, he just assumed I was a chick, and we were down at the river fucking our brains out. So he said, "Have a nice night," and sent us on our way.

But while Jack was talking to the guy, I was looking out over the river. I realized that you could see a house here, a stationary light here, here, and here, and you could pretty much determine exactly where the river was.

You could probably see headlights a mile away. And if you saw one set coming from Mexico and another set coming from the U.S., and they met at the river—or worse, one of the cars just keeps going right across the river—those are smugglers.

We never would have realized that if the guy hadn't pulled us over. But now we knew that nighttime was not the best time to be doing our business. So we started crossing our loads at high noon.

There was a little hilltop that you could get up on with binoculars and a radio, and you could see anybody who was coming. It was actually a pretty unusual place—I mean, the river ran straight as an arrow for miles and miles. But at this one little spot, it makes an S-turn. And if you did your deal at this little spot on the S-turn, nobody on either side of the levee could see you. If any one of us saw any kind of problem, we'd just stay put in Mexico until it was cool to cross.

So that was our place of choice. By now, we were bringing over three or four trucks at a time—nearly 3,000 pounds while the Border Patrol was having lunch.

We had another spot that was very interesting. It was right in the middle of Ascarate Park—a high population area that was close to the river. That was a place we could only use at night. There was an apartment building right up against the levee. It was maybe a hundred units, two stories with a parking lot that backed right up to an irrigation ditch that stayed dry most of the year. We rented an apartment there. We would take a couple of trucks with camper shells and back 'em right up to the ditch at the edge of the parking lot—close to the levee. Hector would go about a quarter-mile down the levee one way and I'd go the other way. We'd make sure it was clear and signal with our radios.

It was like natives in a jungle movie marching down the ditch with bales on their heads. You could barely see them throwing bales into the trucks up above. Fifteen minutes, done. We'd fill up the trucks with bales of pot and just leave them there until morning. Then a couple of our guys would come out wearing hardhats and carrying lunchboxes, get in their trucks and drive off with the regular morning traffic. We'd go and unload it somewhere, and that's how that was done.

JACK STRICKLIN

By now we were starting to make some real money doing 2,000 or 3,000 pounds at a time—three trucks. What we needed was a place to put it. Our stash houses weren't big enough or private enough, and every load had to be weighed and graded before we could send it out. So I went and talked to Bill Holt about using one of his barns.

Bill was a big farmer in the Upper Valley—I knew him through his son Doug. It was his basement where I smoked my first joint. Bill owned a lot of land, but he was cash poor and I knew it. So I went over one day and said, "Bill, I need a place to store some pot. I'll pay you $500 a month for the use of a barn." That was good money in those days. He jumped on it. Bill was a farmer, but he wasn't a dumb farmer. After a while, he saw all that pot going through his barn and started adding it up in his head. It didn't take long before he came to me and said, "Jack, I want to make more than $500 a month."

I said, "What do you want to do?"

"Why don't I set up a deal and we'll split it 50/50?"

I said, "Okay."

Bill knew this pilot who had a hunting ranch down around Chihuahua—a Mexican pilot who would fly hunters in and out. The guy occasionally flew loads and had his own source, but not enough buyers, so Bill came to me about doing something with him.

That guy turned out to be one of the best pilots I ever worked with. He did exactly what he said he would do. He never cheated you. If he told you the load was 576 pounds, it was 576 pounds. And the weed was incredible. It came in square bricks that were wrapped in heavy red and blue paper—our customers called it Christmas wrapping. They couldn't get enough of it.

Bill had his own landing strip out there in the Valley, so this guy would fly in from Chihuahua, and land right there. He flew a Cherokee 6, which could carry anywhere from 600 to 800 pounds. It was an easy deal. We'd run 2,000 or 3,000 pounds across the river in the morning, and that afternoon we'd go unload an airplane.

Our Nashville connect was going strong. I had a guy in Colorado and another one in Florida who were starting to move some weight. We had the best connect in Northern Mexico. Of course, Hector's idea of selling pot was to fucking drown us in it. What are you gonna do? You tell him to stop and he'll find another buyer. Gotta keep feeding the monkey.

I think we were paying about $50 a pound in those days. Selling it for a $100. Had to pay the crew and the drivers out of that, but it still left a decent profit. You're not going to make that kind of money bringing it over on your back—and you'd be facing the same kind of time if you got busted.

You know, my goal was to make $10,000 and then get out. Shit, that was just walkin' around money. I couldn't quit if I wanted to. I was like the dog that finally caught the car. I didn't know exactly what I'd do with it, but I wasn't about to let go.

DOWN MEXICO WAY

I'm not sure Mike and Jack ever took note of the specific moment they crossed the line from ambitious potheads to successful traffickers. But once the dominos began to fall, they quickly found themselves rising to the pinnacle of the border pot trade—though they hardly had time to enjoy the view. They had graduated to tonnage and were opening new markets in the Northeast. They still hadn't found the consistent multi-ton buyer they were looking for, but they were moving better than a ton a week in the high season.

In the early days, the business of pot was all about *Mexican sativa, a* greenish brown plant with little white seeds that provided an excellent high. The only drawback was the incredible exploding seeds. If you didn't remove them, you were in for a surprise that never failed to amuse. But it was great tasting pot with a nice clean high. Not overpowering, but assertive enough to command your full inattention. And the square bricks with the Christmas wrapping coming out of Chihuahua were even better. Mike and Jack got the message: quality matters, presentation sells, customers can be fickle.

Working in his own machine shop, Mike Halliday engineered a faster, easier way to compress loose pot into uniform five-pound bricks. He introduced plastic into the process to preserve freshness and cover the smell. He and Jack sent tools and supplies to Mexico whenever they could. But Mike Halliday couldn't wait to get into the growing fields and launch himself into a process that could benefit from a little of his fine-tuning.

Mike Halliday

The first time Jack and I went to the interior, we didn't know what to expect. When I told a smuggler friend of mine we were going down there he asked me how my Spanish was. "Not too good," I told him. "Why?"

He said, "Just remember the phrase, 'No disparrar a pagar.'" What's that mean? He said, "Don't shoot, I'll pay."

We flew to Mazatlán where we were picked up and taken to Cosala, a little town between Culiacan and Mazatlán, high up in the mountains. The last twenty-five miles is up a windy mountain road that gets you to Cosala. From there, you go on rocky roads barely wide enough for one vehicle. I would ask the guys, "God, doesn't anybody ever die on these roads?"

"Oh, sí, the Gonzalez family, last month they fell off over here and over there."

Jack and I thought we were big-time shit and here we were bouncing around in the back of this old piece-of-crap truck in the dark of night—and I mean dark. By then, we were both pretty pissed off about the whole thing.

We came around one of many hairpin turns where the side of the truck scrapes against the mountain. All of a sudden the truck just stops. The first thing the driver did was kill the lights. I knew what he was going to do—the truck didn't have a starter. He was going to clutch start it in reverse. Not with my ass in it. I put one hand on the rail and got ready to jump off. Jack just looks at me and says, "Mike?"

I said, "WHAT, JACK!" I was pissed.

And he said, "How do you know there is anything down there?"

Sure enough, the driver let it roll backwards just a little

bit, got it started and turned the lights back on. I looked over the side, then I looked at Jack and all I said was, "I'd still be falling."

We spent the night in sleeping bags in the back of the truck. Once the sun came up, we got the full picture of how primitive it was. The workers had nothing but the clothes on their backs—no tools, no trucks—a lot of 'em didn't even have shoes. They moved that shit with homemade handcarts and donkeys. And it was a lot of shit.

Everywhere we looked we saw pot. I mean you can't even comprehend the size of these fields. We'd look at one, and then we'd walk over another hill, and there's another field just as big. It was like wheat in Kansas—it was everywhere. We would buy it by the field. We would go down there and we would just say, "We'll take this field, and that one, and the one over there."

These plants were like fourteen feet high. It was at the end of the growing season—October's the cutting time and these plants were huge. So we were walking along, and all of a sudden our heads turned at the exact same time. About four rows in, there was a plant that looked like nothing else we had ever seen. First of all, the leaves were much darker green. They were obviously the same leaves and everything, but this particular plant had blood-red veins— it was a natural sin semilla (without seeds).

It was the most beautiful pot plant we ever saw. We told the guys that were there, "We want this plant kept separate from everything else, and we'll give you $100." We gave him the $100 right then and there, "Keep this plant separate. I want it taken care of."

When it finally got up to Juarez and Hector saw it, he wouldn't give it to us. He gave us a little bit of it, but he told us, "Fuck no. I ain't giving you this plant."

And I told him "Hector, we paid for it. That's our plant."

He just flat said, "I ain't never seen nothing like this, and I don't care what you want. This is my plant." He did give us some of it, and it was very, very good.

You might think doing business with a Mexican drug lord was something akin to a rattlesnake massage. Not true. If you kept your word, paid your bills, and refrained from cheating, the Mexicans would not only be loyal and generous, but totally invested in keeping you alive. On the other hand, if you didn't deal with them squarely, they would not hesitate to punch your ticket. It was a simple code.

Just as Mike and Jack had been feeling their way along, learning on the job, so had their supplier on the Mexican side, Hector Ruiz-Gonzales. The bloodshed that would mark the ascension of the brutal cartels was still a few years away. Actual violence was surprisingly rare. Hector, in fact, ran his empire without much in the way of competition. He owned the biggest fields and was untouchable—the grandson of la Nacha and heir to the first family of Sinaloa. It's good to be the King.

Mike Halliday spent most of his time in Juarez with Hector. El Paso in the 1970s was not what you'd call cosmopolitan. But the difference made by crossing a river was like riding a time machine twenty years into the past. On the streets of Juarez, law was a rumor, order was an accident, and violence a way of life. On the U.S. side of the border, Mike was just another dealer, living in a modest rental home and blending in with the crowd. But on the wide-open streets of Juarez in the company of the King, he was *Don Miguel,* the powerful *jefe* who resided beyond the reach of law and walked with the swagger of a pistolero.

North of the border, guns were neither necessary nor prudent. It wasn't as if you were going to shoot your way out of trouble. And if anyone got busted, the presence of firearms would only make things worse. Jack Stricklin never took a gun along on the job. There was no need. But to Mike Halliday, a smuggler without a pistol was like a gravedigger without a shovel.

Mike Halliday

Nobody fucked with Hector. The way you could tell his car versus everybody else's car—he didn't have license plates on them. He just drove whatever he wanted. If he felt like stealing a car, he just took it, removed the plates and drove it as long as he liked.

Hector had this beautiful, orange '52 Chevy. One day we were standing on the street right by Fred's Bar, a couple of blocks off the main drag. We were supposed to meet this guy who was gonna show us a load of pot that just came up from the interior. There was nothing much going on, so Hector, myself, and Panchelli were just leaning up against the wall, killing time, waiting for our guy.

This cab pulls up. The driver gets out and starts talking to Hector—he's pretty excited. Some guy had just overdosed on heroin at a bar. The cabbie had his body in the cab and didn't know what to do with him. Hector says, "Ah, fuck, throw him in my trunk." So they opened up the trunk of the car and threw in the body. Then we go back to leaning against the wall waiting for our guy. And here comes Sandy.

Sandy was up from the interior of Mexico. He was somehow or other related to Hector, but hadn't quite yet made his bones. Hector was kind of grooming him.

To this day, I will swear I actually saw a light bulb go off over Hector's head. Hector—he always liked .45s—he pulled out this brand new .45 Gold Cup that I had just given him and said, "Hey Sandy, what do you think of my new gun?"

"Ooh, that's a good gun, man, that's a good gun. I like it."

And Hector said, "You like it? Go ahead and shoot it."

"Okay, where do you want me to shoot it?"

"Shoot it in the trunk."

So the guy walks over to the trunk of the car and *bam*, shoots the .45. "Oh, Hector, that's a good gun—really nice."

"No," Hector says, "Lots of holes, shoot lots of holes."

Well, Sandy empties the clip—*bam, bam, bam, bam, bam, bam, bam,* right into the trunk of that car. Then he hands the gun back. "That's a good gun, Hector."

So Hector took the key and opened the trunk and here's this dead junkie—you could see the holes in the guy. And the traffic is going by—no big deal.

Sandy turns to Hector and says, "Oh, you tricked me— that's a good one, man." And he started laughing so hard Hector had to grab him to keep him from falling over and getting hit by a cab. But if he'd reacted any other way, he'd have been on the next bus back to the interior.

MUSCLE UP

When it came to attracting a loyal band of brothers, Jack Stricklin was the Pied Piper of pot.

As the volume ramped up to several tons a week in the high season, adding muscle became a priority. The crew was assembled organically, more an amorphous assimilation of like-minded friends than a strategically managed expansion. There was no particular aptitude required and just one rule: Thou shalt not snitch. To Jack and Mike, it was the only unpardonable sin. Beyond that, they didn't overburden their guys with lofty expectations. It was a group that responded far better to being aimed than managed.

Jack and Mike trusted their instincts, surrounding themselves with guys who could be counted on to close ranks when the shit hit the fan. These weren't just trained pot monkeys who toted on command, but street-smart, motivated, resourceful contractors who came to the brotherhood with an opportunistic spirit and steadfast loyalty.

Some of them had gone to war believing in duty, honor, and country and come home to the realization that they'd been badly used in a counterfeit cause. Others were friends from the neighborhood and school. Each was connected by the belief that everything they had ever been told by anyone in authority was total bullshit. *The war is just. The government is righteous. Pot is bad. The baby should sleep on its stomach.* What the fuck? Pass the joint.

Jack Stricklin

Johnny Milliorn, ca. 1973

I'd known Johnny Milliorn since high school. He was a hell of a mechanic and one tough son of a bitch. A lot of guys would underestimate him and a lot of guys would get their asses kicked. Johnny would do absolutely anything to win a fight. He grew up with four brothers and it was pretty well known around town that you didn't fuck with the Milliorns.

At the time, Johnny was working in a gas station—barely making it. He had a wife, Karla, and one son, John Jr. But he had no money. None. He hardly made enough to cover rent and groceries. So Mike Halliday and I were at Dave Blott's house one day. And Dave made a joke about me needing a chauffeur with a little hat and a bow tie. He said, "I've got the perfect guy, Johnny Milliorn."

And I thought, you know what? We do need somebody like Johnny. We need muscle. So Dave made a phone call, and about an hour later Johnny showed up. I was the only one that was serious. Everybody else was joking about it. I said, "You want a job?"

And Johnny said, "Yeah."

"Okay, I'll pay you $400 a month and expenses."

"Who do you want me to kill?"

"You drive a car."

"Okay."

"And if we have any problems, you take care of it."

"Okay."

That night I took him home and gave him $400 cash. You can't believe the change that came over this guy. In 1971, $400 was a shitload. So the next day he shows up for work, and I said, "Now you need to go find a car."

"What kind?"

"Well, what kind do you like?"

"I've always wanted a Cadillac."

"Then go buy a Cadillac."

"Where do I get the money?"

"Well, I'll give it to you, Johnny."

So he found a Cadillac, and I bought it. He took care of the trucks and the company cars. He would go collect money, move loads, and if we had a problem with somebody, Johnny would handle it.

You know, everybody talks about the laid-back culture of the pot world and doing business on a handshake—that was mostly true. But everybody in the pot business wasn't Mother Teresa. There were always guys who would rip off loads, steal your customers, and sell you out to the feds in a New York minute.

I made a lot of mistakes in the early days. But one thing I got right: I surrounded myself with a stand-up crew. Not one member of my crew ever turned snitch. The feds knew it. The Mexicans knew it. Other smugglers knew it.

Mike Halliday and I had a policy that if any of our guys ever got busted, we would make their bail, pay the legal fees, and take care of the family while they were away. That's the price of doing business. It would end up costing us a lot of money, but these guys were family. You take care of family.

Mike Halliday

I want to tell you how I met Beto. Beto was my bodyguard—everybody ended up with bodyguards.

After I hooked up with Hector and we started bringing bigger and bigger loads, we would kind of sub out the smaller ones. One night Panchelli tells me he wants to do this particular load. It was only a couple hundred pounds and we weren't all that interested, but Panchelli said, "Let me bring it. I'll get the guys and we'll do it."

So I said, "Okay, no problem."

About 11 o'clock that night, he came to my house and said to me, "I don't know what happened. I dropped the guy off where we always used to cross and told him I'll drive back over the bridge and meet you on the other side. I went around the other side, and I can't find him."

We get in the car and drive down past Fabens where the river is dry as a bone. We walked across shining flashlights—nobody was looking for smugglers in those days. We looked around. We could see where this guy had been walking back and forth. It looked like he'd go a hundred yards, then go back and get a couple bags, go a hundred yards. We started yelling, "Beto! Beto!" But he was long gone. We figured he was probably still in Mexico, walking parallel to the river. We finally gave up and went home.

The next morning Panchelli called me and told me that he had finally heard from him. When the sun started coming up, Beto realized he had never crossed the river, so he finally comes across with the pot and calls Panchelli. I mean you got to be trying real hard to fuck up a simple scam that bad, wandering around all night dragging 200 pounds of pot, with no idea what fucking country you're in. But Beto stayed with the pot and got it across. So we went driving down there one more time and picked him up.

Mike Halliday and his bodyguard, Beto, ca. 1972

I had Panchelli stop on the way to get a six-pack of beer. We found Beto right where he was supposed to be. He had a big smile on his face, which was almost deformed by these huge fucking mosquito bites. He looked like the Elephant Man. We threw the pot in the trunk and headed home.

When I gave Beto a cold one, he acted like I'd just given him a Presidential Rolex. "Oh Mike, thank you so much for the beer. This is the best beer I ever had. Gracias, brother— you are a good friend."

I had never seen anyone so happy! He just kept thanking me and laughing and telling us how funny it was that he got lost at the river.

While I was talking to Beto, I noticed one of his fingers looked like he had a big ass mushroom growing out of it—a huge thing. It turns out that Beto worked as a meat cutter at a butcher shop in Juarez. When Panchelli came by and told him he wanted him to help with the load—well, Beto had always wanted to get in the business but never got the chance. So when Panchelli told him he had a job for him, Beto was over the moon.

"Oh Mike, this is a really good beer. Thank you."

I couldn't take my eyes of his finger. I had to ask, "Beto, what the fuck happened to your finger there?"

Everything was a joke to him. He started laughing again and said, "Yesterday, after Panchelli tell me about the job, I got so excited I cut my finger off—pretty funny, huh?"

"Beto, that looks kind of serious, bro."

"Maybe I see a doctor."

Jesus, the guy cuts off his finger, wraps a little gauze around it, hauls 200 pounds of pot around all night, gets eaten alive by mosquitos, and all he can do is laugh about it. I realized he had a big set of stones on him.

And from that moment on, Beto was my bodyguard.

L to R: Lee Chagra and Jack Stricklin, ca. 1973

THE BLACK STRIKER

Lee Chagra was a well-known defense attorney, a shameless self-promoter and a gambler of legendary proportions. What Lee Chagra was *not* was a drug lord. Though he may have prowled the grey areas of the law and undoubtedly crossed the line on frequent occasions, he did not traffic in marijuana. Lee Chagra didn't even smoke marijuana in the early days, though cocaine would ultimately become one of his many mistresses.

Yet Lee would live his life with a target on his back, affixed from the moment he began to associate with Jack Stricklin and Mike Halliday. As their lawyer and confidante, he was privy to a lot of the nuts and bolts of their operation. But the DEA was so certain he was the man turning the wrench, they would have granted immunity to Satan himself if he would give testimony against Lee Chagra.

With his oversized personality, Lee sucked up attention like a black hole, casting his super-sized ego upon everything he touched, including the operation run by Jack and Mike. The Justice Department was so blinded by his outlaw image that they couldn't believe anyone else could be calling the shots. They needed a suitable villain to justify the legitimacy of their cause. And they were convinced beyond doubt that Lee Chagra was the man. Mike and Jack couldn't know it at the time, but the attorney they paid so handsomely to defend them would only add to the heat that was threatening to bring them down.

JACK STRICKLIN

> The only reason we met Lee Chagra was we knew we were going to need a lawyer sooner or later. Dave Blott thought we should go to Sib Abraham, but I didn't really trust Sib, so I said, "How about this Lee Chagra?"
>
> Right about this same time Tommy Pitts, our Nashville buyer, came to town and got busted with some of his crew. They were sloppy—called too much attention to themselves. An agent picked up on it and followed a truckload of pot to a little place they kept for when they were in town. So he called it in and got a warrant.
>
> I had gone to the house to see if I could settle these guys down. Shit, they had a truck half-filled with pot sitting outside their door, and they were acting like idiots. I actually walked out the back door of that house, got in my car, and was driving off when the feds kicked in the front door. That's how close I came to getting busted. Well, they needed a lawyer real quick, and so I said to Mike, "Go see Lee Chagra."

Mike Halliday

I went down to Lee Chagra's office. He answered the door with a gun in his hand, because it was late at night. I introduced myself and told him what was going on and he said he could get the guys out, but it was gonna cost $10,000. I said, "No problem." I reached down and pulled $5,000 out of my right boot and $5,000 out of my left boot and threw it on his desk.

I don't think Lee had ever been paid that way before. He had this kind of stunned look on his face, like, "Who are you?" But there was $10,000 in cash sitting on his desk, and that got his attention.

It's one of those stories that kind of got blown out of proportion. In the book *Dirty Dealing*, the writer (Gary Cartwright) had somebody else throwing the money on Lee's desk. But it was me. And according to that book, after I threw out the $10,000, Lee said, "Oh, it's $10,000 apiece," and I just keep throwing out more money. But that's not how it happened. He got it wrong. If his version was true, I would have needed bigger boots.

As Mike Halliday and Jack Stricklin became adept at piling up large sums of cash, it was apparent they had little idea how to deal with it. They put most of their money in closets and under beds. Mike bought a classic '59 XLCH Harley Sportster, Jack a Jaguar XKE. They threw their cash around like confetti, acquiring enough bling to embarrass the Klondike. But beyond that, their abundant cash was just another way to tally the score.

Through Lee Chagra, they purchased 250 acres on the San Juan River in Farmington, New Mexico; a racehorse named For the Road; a twenty-five acre trailer park, a bar, and a small fleet of trucks, sports cars, and motorcycles. Lee advised them to file tax returns based on their right to claim the source of their income as "Privileged Information." You didn't have to look too hard to find the headwaters of their assets. But Jack and Mike were paying enough in taxes to stay on the good side of the IRS, the only feds they were truly afraid of.

These were all things any decent attorney could have done. But Lee Chagra's most valuable asset was his vast network. He knew everyone who mattered, with friends on all sides of the law—judges, prosecutors, clerks, cops, bondsmen. These were his drinking and gambling buddies, his pipeline to the judicial system. The grand jury couldn't send out for coffee without Lee Chagra knowing about it.

Just as he was lending sophistication to the enterprise, Mike Halliday and Jack Stricklin were transforming Lee Chagra from a crusading defense lawyer into a wealthy drug lawyer. He often referred to the impressive home he was building in El Paso's upper valley as *The House that Jack Built*. It was not by accident that he failed to credit Mike Halliday.

Lee Chagra was one of the few issues on which Mike and Jack disagreed. But there's no doubt that behind the glittering veil was a skilled and effective attorney. He was the star of whatever courtroom he entered and loved nothing more than to spit in the eye of the all-powerful Government. His trials were "must see" events—choreographed by a gifted showman who dominated the stage like a high-stepping rock star.

A new kind of criminal was filling the courts—the oxymoronic felon, perpetrator of the victimless crime. Without a sympathetic victim to parade in front of juries, the Government began to rely on snitches. There were always those who were more than willing to flip in exchange for reduced time. And if none could be coerced, one or two could certainly be manufactured. It was a self-perpetuating cycle, fueling the engine of a hot new industry called drug enforcement. If you didn't have a lawyer who could play dirty, you didn't have a chance.

Okay, let me tell you about the first time I got in trouble. I had a yellow International Scout—not the one Jack brought home. I bought a used one. The title wasn't in my name, of course. But everybody knew it was my Scout. I drove it everywhere. It was yellow too, and it was beefed up.

The keywords in this whole story are "International Scout."

Beto—he loved that Scout, and he wanted to use it to smuggle small loads. I wouldn't let him because even though it wasn't registered in my name, the feds knew whose Scout it was. But Beto kept on me about it, so one day I just gave up and went to a notary public and had the vehicle transferred to him. That same day, I went down to the International dealership and bought a brand-spanking-new blue-and-white International Scout. It was beautiful.

So Beto gets the old Scout. That thing would hold about 700 pounds packed in there pretty good. I told him to be careful. But man, you just couldn't talk sense to that guy. He decided he's gonna take the Scout and bring 700 pounds across the damn river—all by himself. He doesn't need people standing watch for him or monitoring the scanners or anything else.

Of course, he brings that load across the river at night and runs straight into the Border Patrol. And off they go down the highway in a high-speed chase. Beto decides the only way he's gonna get out of this is to get back to Mexico. So he goes off the road and heads for the river. He sees a spot that looks pretty good, drops down from the levee, and just flies out into the river.

Of course, he crashes the Scout and the pot ends up everywhere. He broke a few ribs, but he still got out of the vehicle. And he runs for the Mexican side, shooting over his shoulder. Beto loved to shoot that fucking gun.

He ended up getting away, but they still had the Scout and all the pot. And they figured out pretty fast that the Scout belonged to me. Well, they got real excited about that. "We're finally gonna get Mike Halliday!"

The next night, I'm coming across the border in my brand new Scout, right? As soon as they saw me about five cars away, they started waving everybody through until they got to me. The guy tells me to get out of the car and keep my hands in sight. So I got out and they put my hands on the hood and snapped on the cuffs. They were practically celebrating.

They drug my ass off into a room, and this FBI guy comes in and starts asking questions. I tell him right away I want a lawyer and he lets me call Lee Chagra. The Fed was a straight-up guy. He figured out pretty fast I wasn't going to tell him anything.

It turns out they had jumped the gun on my arrest. Jamie Boyd was the U.S. Magistrate, and he hated my ass. When my name came up he said, "Go get him right now!" But it turns out the only thing they could charge me with was not carrying a draft card. In those days, you had to have it on you at all times. I was classified 4A—married with dependents. I wasn't even eligible for the draft. But they charged me anyway and let me make a call to Lee Chagra.

The road at that bridge was one-way going into the U.S. The only way you could get on it was by driving across to Juarez and coming back through customs. But here comes this black Cadillac down the road the wrong way—and pulls right into the checkpoint. Lee Chagra gets out of the car in his fucking pajamas and bedroom slippers, walks up to the first cop he sees and says, "Where's my client?"

So they bring him to me, and he makes a phone call to some judge, then hangs up the phone and tells the agents the judge said to let me go.

"Let him go?"

"Yeah, he's been released on his own recognizance. He'll be in court tomorrow." They weren't very happy about it, but all they really had was the draft card thing

The next day, I was at Lee's office getting ready to go over to the courthouse where I was going to go before Jamie Boyd. I told Lee I had papers to prove I had sold the Scout the day before, but he told me not to say anything about it. So we went over to the courthouse and Lee runs into the prosecutor. Lee told him, "Let's go get a cup of coffee before this thing starts." And off they went.

So a little while later we're standing in front of the judge, and the prosecutor asks, "Mr. Halliday, do you have a draft card?"

"Yes sir, I do."

"Then why didn't you have it in your possession when you were stopped at the bridge?"

"I didn't think I needed to carry it. But I'll have it with me from now on."

"I have no further questions, your honor."

Well, Jaime Boyd just flipped out. "What do you mean you don't have any more questions? I got some questions for him!"

And he looked at me and he says, "Mr. Halliday, can you look me in the eye and tell me you have never owned a yellow 1968 International Travelall?"

I looked him right straight in the eye and I said, "Your honor, I have never owned a yellow 1968 International Travelall."

Now, if he had said "Scout," I would have never been able to keep a straight face.

Jaime Boyd was so fucking mad he just told everybody to get out of his courtroom—just go! So I left with Lee and we were walking across the street to his office and I asked, "How in the world did you ever pull that one off?"

Lee just reached into his pocket and pulled out his

solid gold fifty-peso money clip and showed me that it was empty—not one bill. Lee always carried at least $1,000 in that thing.

While Lee Chagra crafted his image through high-profile drug cases, he refined it in the casinos of Las Vegas. He was an addicted gambler whose junkets were legendary. Lee was wined, dined, and entertained at the expense of the casino. A separate blackjack table was cordoned off just for him. He would play a hand at every position, winning or losing hundreds of thousands of dollars in a single night.

To Lee Chagra, beating the casino was like beating the Government. He craved the action and attention with equal measure. When he walked into the casino, heads turned. The promenade to his private table was lined with backslappers—fellow gamblers who stopped down to see "The Black Striker" in action. And Lee loved every second of it. Casting the image of a rakish outlaw, he strode confidently through his incandescent playground, sporting a big black Stetson, a walking stick dipped in gold, and a smile that could charm the tick off a dog's ass.

Jack Stricklin

We started going with Lee to Las Vegas. They'd send a Lear Jet for him, everything would be on the house. Lee was very well known in that town.

One night I walked up to the blackjack table and asked, "Who is this table reserved for?"

They said, "The Chagra party."

I said, "I'm in the Chagra party."

The guy said, "Sit down."

Well, I blow through $8,000 in about ten minutes.

The next thing you know, here comes Lee walking

through the casino with a hooker. And he says, "Where you going?"

"Oh, I'm going to the room and go to bed. I just blew $8,000."

"No, wait a minute. Don't get excited."

So Lee sits down, lays out the chips and five minutes later, he gets up and hands me $8,000. He says, "Now you feel better?"

That was Lee. On the one hand he could be very generous, on the other hand he had the morals of a rattlesnake. He'd fuck your wife. He'd fuck you. He had no scruples, which I suppose is what made him such a damn good lawyer. But that's all he was—our lawyer. The idea that he was running our business was bullshit.

Of course, Lee would die before the feds ever quit trying to prove it.

ANATOMY OF AN OUTLAW

Much like Prohibition in the 1930s, the legislative attempt to control a small problem only created a bigger one. Alcohol went underground and criminal organizations flourished. It would be simplistic to presume that organized crime was merely the result of overreaching legislation. But it was clearly a byproduct. Fifty years later, as pot gained traction among the Baby Boomers, the curtain came up on the second act of Prohibition. And once again, a new class of criminal emerged.

The outlaw lifestyle was alive and well in El Paso in the early '70s. Not to say Mike, Jack, and the crew were totally lawless, just a bit more discriminating about the laws they chose to observe. They were perpetrating an act as non-violent as raiding the refrigerator. Criminals hurt people. They sold pot. And if pot was a tonic for unhappy times, it couldn't have come along at a more appropriate moment.

We had lost the war in Vietnam. The Arabs were threatening our oil supply. America was hip-deep in the worst economic collapse since the Great Depression. Rioters and looters took to the streets. Four students were killed by National Guard troops on the campus of Kent State. Widespread corruption stained every level of government. And to top it off, the Comet Kohoutek was on a collision course with the Planet Earth and the Killer Bees were coming.

If you wanted to find the crew, you wouldn't have to look much further than the Desert Lounge, a bar jointly owned by Mike and Jack. It was totally generic—from its neon beer signs and formica tabletops to the pool table and pickled eggs. The bar probably gave away more beer than it sold—it was really just a glorified clubhouse. I hung out there from time to time

L to R: Mike Halliday and Jimmy Milliorn, ca. 1973

and was always welcomed. If you're a friend of Jack Stricklin, you're a friend of the crew.

By that time, I had known Jack for nearly ten years. As I grew up, he occupied a semi-permanent stool in our kitchen. He was a favorite of my sisters and younger brother, not to mention my mother and the Colonel, who always welcomed him warmly. Everybody liked Jack Stricklin, even those who didn't totally approve of how he made his living.

To me, Jack was like a big brother. I admired him for the certainty and confidence with which he lived his life. He played by a strict set of rules and provided a commodity that was in high demand. In typical Jack fashion, he stripped away all the legal issues and cut to the obvious conclusion that there was nothing wrong with smoking pot. Everybody wanted it, and somebody had to go and get it. It might as well be him.

Occasionally, Jack would throw me a kilo, and I would break it up and sell it to friends. It was a small taste of the life, just enough to keep me on the outer edge of the circle. Jack made it clear there was a place for me if I wanted in. But I was pursuing my own ambition, and it never seemed compatible with a felony conviction. I was content with the occasional trip to the Desert Lounge and a ringside seat at the edge of the insurrection.

You could usually find Johnny Milliorn holding court at the bar, if not tending the bar. To look at Johnny, you would think he was anything but a tough guy. He had a Homer Simpson body and a hairline headed south. I never once saw him in jeans. Polyester was his fabric of choice. He looked more like a man who should be selling *Snap-On Tools* than enforcing for Jack.

The oldest of five brothers, Johnny grew up on a diet of knuckles and blood. The Milliorns communicated with their fists. When they grew tired of beating the shit out of each other, they turned their attention to the street, where fighting was a popular pastime. "Let's go pick some shit" was as much a part of a Friday night as high-school football.

Johnny didn't come to the business with the high-minded ideology of a revolutionary. Nor was he particularly concerned about the hypocrisy of government. He needed a job. With a wife and kids to support, there wasn't much of a future in street fighting. So Jack Stricklin gave Johnny a cause and was rewarded with a man who quickly surpassed the role of goon and became an important asset and trusted friend.

There were others, of course. Some were family, like Johnny's brother, Jimmy, a tough guy who wanted to let everybody know he was a tough guy. A former member of the Bandidos motorcycle club, Jimmy had a face like a toothache and wore a toupee that would slip and slide across his head like a runaway dust bunny. But pity the man who would dare to notice out loud.

A number of the crew were veterans like Buzzy Harrison, just out of the Navy and possessed of a technical aptitude that proved critical to the mechanics of a successful smuggle; and

Mickey Malone, a former Army paratrooper who had fought in Vietnam and returned to the world with a fondness for good pot and a craving for adrenaline.

The treatment of our returning vets may have been the biggest shame of Vietnam. One minute our troops were at war with a fiercely committed foe, the next they were struggling to find their place in a country that was at war with itself. Barely out of their teens, they were sent forth to kill and returned to a divided nation that did little or nothing to ease a significant transition.

Unlike some of the loudest political voices of the time, Jack Stricklin and Mike Halliday didn't confuse an immoral war with those who fought it. Veterans came to the business of pot highly motivated and well prepared. For those who happened to be friends of Mike or Jack, a place was always found. Vets were the best among their crew—and the least likely to render aid to a government that held so little of their respect.

Prominent among the crew was William Russell—known to his friends as Billy. The stepson of a retired Army Master Sergeant, Billy grew up with Mike Halliday in El Paso's Lower Valley. He chased his fun like any typical El Paso teenager, but he avoided serious trouble and tended to the obligations of home and school. Billy Russell would be the first in his family to attend college, and one more in a long line of distracted students who would sacrifice their academic eligibility for the sake of a good party.

After flunking out of college, Billy Russell's fate was in the hands of the local draft board. But he wouldn't wait around to be drafted. He was a patriot—God, Honor, Country to his core. Billy volunteered for helicopter flight school and distinguished himself at every level of training. In 1967, he was ordered to Vietnam, where the lifespan of a helicopter pilot was measured in weeks.

For every twenty-five hours flown under hostile fire, the Army awarded an Air Medal. During his thirteen-month tour of duty in Vietnam, Chief Warrant Officer William H. Russell earned twenty-one Air Medals, plus the Distinguished Flying Cross, the Bronze Star and the Purple Heart. His role in the Vietnam War was a remarkable testament to courage, if not the perfect recipe for a committed confederate of the Pot Rebellion.

BILLY RUSSELL

I had some 700 hours under fire. That's why I came home crazy. Now, it wasn't always that intense. They didn't always hit us. But they were shooting at us—they were definitely shooting at us. I was shot down multiple times. I'd come back full of holes, leaking fuel, hydraulics failing. "Where can I put it down while I still have the option?" That was considered a shoot-down. Of course, a couple of times, I just crashed—literally just crashed the aircraft. They don't give you any medals for that.

I remember the first Tet Offensive. I was down south still flying gunships, doing combat assaults all over that area, and that's the day I got shot. I got into a gunfight with somebody in a concrete pillar—a pillbox. I was trying to put a rocket right into that pillbox and the slit is only about a foot high. I kept shooting at it with rockets. I know I'm gonna get one in there and I kept flying, and all of a sudden I hear my wingman in the earphones, "Break, break, break!"

Well, I'm trying to get away from the target and they put twenty rounds through the belly of my helicopter. One of them hit the bottom of my seat and proceeded to go right through my ankle. It actually knocked me off the controls in the middle of a critical turn—thank God my copilot was on top of it. He grabbed the controls immediately and flew me straight back to our home base, five or six minutes away.

They strapped my ass to a gurney, put me on a chopper, and flew me to Nha Trang where the hospital was. They operated on my right leg—took out a shitload of shrapnel. That's how I got the Purple Heart.

The thing of it was though, all that stuff I got medals for wasn't nearly as hairy as what I did up around Khe Sanh. But there wouldn't be any medals for those missions—no recognition whatsoever. Because according to all official records, they never happened—we were never there.

I was assigned to an A Team Unit. They didn't tell me this at the time. They just told me where to go. I had a heavy-fire team plus one, which is four gunships and two Hueys—six helicopters. We took off, flew north forever until we located this little place called Hue/Phu Bai, which is south of the Imperial City of Hue, right on the Demilitarized Zone between North and South Vietnam. We landed there and I reported to the commanding officer of the unit. He briefed me about what they were doing, and I asked, "Why are all these other people here?"

And he says, "We have 500 mercenaries here called Nungs. They're Cambodian, Laotian, Chinese—experienced fighters. What we do is we take a team of Special Forces guys and Nungs and insert them into locations you'll be given after you fly to Khe Sanh."

Khe Sanh is on the other border to the west. It's a scary place, under constant mortar and artillery attacks. They were almost overrun numerous times. So I get there and the CO says, "We have intel that there's a regiment of NVA right here—X marks the spot."

I see right away that the spot is inside of North Vietnam. "You mean we're going to go in and put these eleven guys right in the middle of a regiment of the North Vietnamese Regular Army?"

"Yes Mr. Russell, that's exactly what you're going to do."

I was immediately struck with a certainty that these would be my last days. I had never had that sense the entire time I was in Vietnam. But from that moment I figured I would die in a place the Government wouldn't even admit I'd ever been.

We stayed at Phu Bai with the Nungs. I learned how truly badass those guys really were. Every man I saw walked around barefoot in a loincloth. And every one of them had multiple gunshot wounds, scars all over them. They had the look of death in their eyes.

The Special Forces A Team were serious troops—not a Hollywood thing, they were the real deal. They were hand-picked, elite, and they were all killers. They were working with the Nungs who got extra pay for the number of kills they made. So they were highly motivated. The Nungs wore the ears of dead enemies around their necks on leather thongs. When they dressed up to go into battle, I'd never seen anything like it. They carried so many weapons—multiple pistols and rifles and so much ammunition—these were little people, at least in height. But in full gear, they had to weigh over 300 pounds apiece. The Hueys, or slicks as we called them, carried 5,000 rounds of M60 ammunition for each gun, plus the crew chief and a door gunner on each side. My gunship carried as much ammunition as I could hover with. And I would fly from Phu Bai west up to Khe Sanh, which lies in a valley between mountains.

Our job was to insert these teams to determine the enemy's level of occupation—a regimental-size unit or a division—whatever it was. Of course, there were times when there was nothing there. But most of the time it was hot. We'd put those guys on the ground and they'd fight their way out of the landing zone.

On approach, there were four gunships, two on each side of those two slicks. We had two A1E's—propeller-driven airplanes with 250-pound bombs and 50-caliber machine guns on the wing. They prepped the landing zone and flew cover while a pair of F-4s circled up above. During each insertion, we expended every single round and every rocket we had to get those guys in there, because the fighting was usually that fierce. I'm talking about 10,000 rounds of ammunition in short order. Our mission was to drop them and then go back to Khe Sanh as fast as we could, rearm and refuel and wait for the call to pick them up.

The extraction was even hairier. When we went to pick them up, we went in fast, shooting everything we had at everybody we could, and we were taking heavy fire every time. When the guys on the ground made contact with the size unit they were looking for, they were in communication with an airbase in Guam. They'd deploy six B-52s, armed with 2,000-pound bombs with a quarter-second delay, which meant that the bomb

CWO William Russell on his return from Vietnam in 1968

would penetrate the ground seventeen feet before it went off. Those bombs made a crater that you could hide a 48-foot rotor disk Huey down inside of.

Once we picked them up and reached the IP—that initial point which meant I was clear of the area—I would key the mic to a certain frequency and let the bombers know we were clear. They would rain hell from the sky. You can imagine how much ordinance was put down by a flight of six B-52s.

Most of the time, those guys had to fight their way in and

out of the Landing Zone, and that's when those A1E's saved our ass. They were dropping bombs and raising hell with those 50-cals. There were times when we picked up those guys with blood coming out of their noses and ears. They were calling the bombs down right on top of themselves. And there were wounded guys, and they were charged up like you just would not believe. I think my nerves were on edge the better part of fifteen years after those incidents.

Anything I ever did in Vietnam, before or after that, paled by comparison to what we did up in Khe Sanh. Every day was life or death intensity—you had to treat it like that—no half steps. If you shot at me, I chased you down and killed you. The worst thing you can do is to flinch or back off when somebody's zeroing in on you. What you do is you turn to do battle with them. If you have the slightest hesitation about what you're doing, you're dead.

THE GOLDEN SPIKE

Billy Russell never smoked pot in Vietnam. He was a squared-away Army aviator whose high of choice was the adrenaline rush of combat. Though the Army dangled the prospects of a full commission and sweetened the pot with a prestigious assignment to Corps Headquarters at Gray Army Airfield, Fort Hood, Billy knew that any promises he received would be contingent on a second tour in Vietnam. What came next would settle any question of reenlistment.

In the summer of 1968, CWO William Russell was assigned to the U.S. Secret Service. Along with several other pilots and 25,000 troops trained for riot control, he was ordered to Chicago to help keep the peace at the National Democratic Convention, where an unhappy riot of activists had congregated to express their feelings about everything from civil rights to the war in Vietnam.

Billy Russell navigated the narrow canyons of downtown Chicago and witnessed police beating back protesters with clubs and water cannons. Then he would alter course and discover protesters outnumbering and overpowering the police. In a matter of weeks, he had gone from flying assault missions against an enemy of democracy in a faraway country, to providing air cover at a national party convention in America's heartland. It was a dawning point.

While the war in Vietnam would eventually obliterate the remnants of Billy Russell's patriotism, he didn't exhibit his anger like an open wound. He was a pillar of self-discipline. But just beneath the surface simmered the conflict of a soldier who had experienced first-hand the intensity of war—and relished the experience. Thanks to Uncle Sam, Billy Russell was ready-made for the business of pot. Adrenaline was his bitch, and he was about to discover the golden spike.

BILLY RUSSELL

In 1972, I had been out of the Army a couple of years and had just gotten my degree. I was married, had a son, and was working as an industrial equipment salesman for the petroleum industry.

I was smoking pot then, and that was what really changed my perspective about what I did in Vietnam. The Government turned me into a killer and was willing to waste my life on the basis of a lie. I believed then—and I still believe—that the pot laws were wrong. Just like the Vietnam War was wrong. It's funny how fast I changed after I started smoking pot. I realized the war was never going to be won. The Government was totally corrupt. And I was a pissed-off veteran. I still loved my country. But I hated my government. Still, Mike and Jack were messing with them in a serious way. And they had a serious way of messing with you right back.

I hadn't completely crossed the line. I helped Mike Halliday now and then. We grew up together in the Lower Valley, and I could always count on him for good pot. One day he came to me about delivering a load to Tennessee. So I rented a car, put a U-Haul trailer on it and drove it to Murfreesboro. I was paid $5 a pound for transporting it—1,000 pounds. So I drove it over there and dropped it off, cleaned out the trailer, returned the U-Haul and the rental car, jumped on an airplane and flew back to El Paso. In a single weekend, I made

$5,000. And in 1972, I was making $300 a week. All of a sudden, in a couple of days, I made $5,000. That got my attention.

After that, Mike started talking to me more and more about what he was doing. They were bringing pot over by the ton and distributing to some pretty big clients. But they needed help transporting it. They liked the fact that I had short hair and looked like a straight arrow.

So one day Mike took me down to his house on Lafayette Street in the Lower Valley and he said, "I'll show you where to go and get it. Just bring the U-Haul, we'll load you up, and you'll be gone in fifteen minutes."

I knew how easy it was, but I also knew the risk. I had a family and a job. We were living month to month, but we were doing a lot better than we would if I went to prison. Anyway, Mike took me to this double closet there in the house and opened up the sliding doors. Sitting on the floor was a suitcase. He told me to open it. It was filled with neatly bundled stacks of cash—about $300,000.

I was just taken aback by that. Here was a kid four or five years younger than me—a kid who didn't really have what I considered bright prospects. I mean, he was a nice kid, but he was always running into trouble when he was younger. We just kind of considered him a tagalong.

And here I am, standing in his house in the Lower Valley, looking at a suitcase on his closet floor, and there's $300,000 in it. My whole opinion of the man changed in that instant. And it was like, "My God, I'm in. I'm totally in!" That's all it took. I can still feel the treble hook sinking deep.

In 1973, Richard Nixon upped his game, putting an end to the alphabet-soup approach to drug enforcement and combining the BNDD and several incompatible organizations under the single brand of the United States Drug Enforcement Administration.

Nixon endowed his fledgling DEA with the authority to take the war to the street and put an end to rampant drug abuse, by which he largely meant marijuana. It was becoming a hot political issue. He hoped it might deflect some of the attention away from the emerging scandal of Watergate. Unfortunately for Mr. Nixon, merging several large organizations into one may look good on paper, but what normally ensues is something akin to a shift-change at the knucklehead factory.

The DEA began their existence as the Justice Department equivalent of a bad comb-over—looked okay from a distance, but the closer you got, the more apparent the illusion. With a budget just shy of $74 million and fewer than 1,500 special agents nationwide, the fledgling DEA was underfunded and overmatched, making do with hand-me-down vehicles and equipment, inexperienced agents and insufficient funds. But despite the fact that it was early in the game, the El Paso DEA was on to Jack Stricklin from Day One.

To say that Jack wasted little effort to conceal the source of his lifestyle would be an understatement. In fact, he perpetuated his outlaw image, adding spice to the menudo with a measure of gamesmanship that would further motivate the emerging DEA. As much as Jack loved the money, he relished the rush. To him, it was a glorious game of cat and mouse. And Jack Stricklin rarely passed up an opportunity to remind the DEA exactly who was the mouse.

JACK STRICKLIN

> I never considered the DEA to be my enemy. The laws they were trying to enforce were my enemy, but the DEA was mostly just guys doing a job. There were a few agents I got to know, like Nap Herrera and J.T. Robinson. They were DEA agents, but they were straight-up DEA agents. They would

try as hard as they could to bring you down, but that was business. If they did bust you, they knew you weren't going to put up a fight. So there was kind of an understanding and respect between us. They'd even come into the bar and have a drink now and then. We'd always find something to laugh about.

The El Paso DEA really didn't have a chance in those early days. We had faster cars, bigger trucks, better airplanes—we had the best radios and scanners. We even had one of the first night-vision scopes ever made. I got it in a drug deal from a guy at Motorola—it was a prototype.

We were better organized and had more money. All the feds had were a bunch of guys from the East Coast they brought in to follow us around—they stood out like a whore in church. And they knew nothing about the local highways or desert roads.

One day, Johnny Milliorn and I are driving around in my Jaguar, and he started looking around, and he said, "Okay, there's one, there's one. What are we going to do?"

I said, "Well, let's show 'em around."

Where I-10 goes past UTEP and makes that sweeping curve to the east—right there in the middle of that curve I was doing about 110. I looked in the rear-view mirror. These guys were driving an old Ford. They had that thing on two wheels! I had to slow down so they wouldn't kill themselves. I'd let 'em catch up, then I'd floor it again. We gave 'em a tour of both valleys and everything in between.

Not too long after that, I walked into the bar and Napoleon Herrera is sitting there drinking a beer. He says, "Hey, Jack, can I talk to you for a minute?"

I said, "Sure Nap, what's up?"

"Listen," he says, "you've got to quit driving that fucking Jaguar so fast. Those guys nearly flipped that old Ford coming through downtown. Somebody dies, and they're going to hit your ass with a murder charge."

It was all a big joke—cops and robbers—only the cops didn't have any money. We'd fill up the car and run it out of gas, fill it up and do it again. And they're right behind us all the way, trying to scrape together gas money to stay in the game.

By 1973, Jack Stricklin didn't have a lot of time to worry about the DEA. He was up to his ass in the day-to-day operation of a multi-million dollar import business. How do you maintain margins without losing clients? How do you keep the crew busy and out of trouble? Hector wants to keep sending product and you can't afford to say no, but where do you put it? Stash houses have to be found and secured. Product has to be moved between buyers. Suitcases filled with cash have to be safely transferred. As one prominent advertiser is quick to point out, *it's logistics,* whatever the fuck that is.

But whatever it was, Jack was good at it. He spent every day driving around with Johnny Milliorn. He wore a beeper and was never without a roll of quarters. He moved from pay phone to pay phone, making calls, and keeping all the details in his head. He kept no books. If you asked him how much weight he had sent to a buyer, he couldn't tell you. He didn't think in terms of weight, he thought in terms of dollars. Jack knew to the penny how much money he was owed. He organized loads, force-fed whatever clients he could, ran the crew, managed the payables and receivables, and kept the DEA out of his rear-view mirror. In constant motion but never in a hurry, Jack Stricklin put in a full day at the office, which dovetailed nicely with the full nights he devoted to crossing his loads.

The early days of the pot rebellion were more a reflection of the counterculture that inspired it than of the bloodbath it would become. The operation run by Jack and Mike was 100% based on trust. Hundreds of thousands of dollars worth of pot was exchanged on a handshake, and everyone was paid in full. There was no hate. Guns were more or less contained to the Mexican side, and violence was rarely a threat. Everyone understood that the same risk was assumed for selling a ton of pot as an ounce. Five years was the prescribed penalty—eighteen months with good behavior. So the object of the game was tonnage. And the game was ever changing.

JACK STRICKLIN

Tommy Pitts and John Wheeler were our Tennessee buyers. They were our first big buyers—we'd been doing business for a couple of years. They had a customer of their own in Atlanta named John Hughes. He was their biggest buyer, and they couldn't keep up with him. No matter how much they sent him, he always wanted more. The guy was a black hole, he moved everything he got and paid it off in ten days. But Tommy and John didn't have the organization to handle what he needed.

I knew it. And I knew that sooner or later they were going to either lose him or give him to us. So finally, they came to us and said, "We can't handle him. He's yours if you want him."

Are you kidding me? A multi-ton buyer who pays off in ten days and sells everything you can send him? "Okay, we'll take him off your hands. No problem." John Hughes immediately became our biggest buyer.

John was gay. He lived with his mother, and he was an absolute perfectionist—everything he touched had to be just perfect—he was like Felix in the *Odd Couple*. Every dollar I ever collected from him came sunny-side up—perfectly bundled, accurate to the penny. He was just what we were looking for, but there was no way I was ever going to let him push me for product like he did to Tommy Pitts and John Wheeler. I wanted to make sure he knew I was a one-stop shop. So I took a page out of Hector's book and fucking drowned the guy in pot.

Well, John finally called me one day, and he said, "Jack, I'm taking a break. I don't want any more weed. Fuck you. I'm tired, and I'm stressed. I'll call you when I'm ready to get back to work. Don't call me. Goodbye." And he hung up.

So about a month later, he calls me and says, "Okay, I'm fresh, I'm ready. Go ahead and send it. The house will be open. Just go ahead and put it in the house."

"How much do you want me to send?"

"Send me all you've got."

"Are you sure?"

"Bring it."

Well, we had just brought in 6,000 pounds, so I sent Billy Russell down there in a U-Haul. I flew to Atlanta with Johnny to help him unload at John's mother's house. By the time we were through, there was pot in every room of that house—floor to ceiling—even in his mother's bedroom.

The next thing I know, John Hughes is calling me, "What the fuck is wrong with you? My mother's bedroom is full of weed!"

"You told me the house was open and you said to send all we could send."

He said, "How much is it?"

I said, "6,000 pounds."

He got real quiet for a minute and then he said, "Come back in ten days. I'll have your payment".

Ten days later, Billy and I flew down and collected it.

SNITCHED

Mike Halliday

You know, the DEA wasn't stupid. Well, some of them were, but they had some smart ones too, and they knew exactly what we were doing. But in those days, you almost had to get caught in the act for any chance of a conviction, and we were careful to make sure that didn't happen. But Dave Blott was a lazy son of a bitch. He always wanted to cut corners. He did everything half-assed and was one of those guys out for himself. He missed a crossing one time because he'd rather play poker—the guy wanted to be a big-time drug dealer, but he didn't want to work at it.

Dave didn't like the fact that I was getting better shit from Hector than he could get from any of his people. So he comes to Jack and me one day and he says, "I got a guy who can get a better product than Hector, at a better price."

"Okay fine, whatever—if you want to try getting better stuff, go ahead."

And so we bought him a truck—a brand new U-Haul type truck with a box on the back, completely enclosed. And we gave him $200,000 to do the deal. He was supposed to get around 3,000 pounds.

Well, the 3,000 pounds he got was every pound of pot that the El Paso DEA had busted up to that point. The DEA gets Dave, they get credit for busting the 3,000 pounds all over again, they get the truck, and they get our $200,000—everything. It was big headlines in the paper—the biggest bust in the history of El Paso. They told the whole story how the DEA shut down a huge drug ring. But the fact is, not a single word was ever printed about the $200,000—not a word. The cops got that.

And so Dave went off to La Tuna, which was kind of fine with Jack and me because he wasn't doing a fucking thing anyway. And we could get back to our world without having to worry about him.

Dave's bust and the loss of $200,000 was barely a hiccup as far as Mike Halliday and Jack Stricklin were concerned—a small price to pay for streamlining the division of labor. Their prodigious run continued unabated over the next eighteen months. The addition of John Hughes in Atlanta placed them at the top of the northern border's fastest growing industry. And they never broke stride.

While Jack played the entrepreneur, Mike spent most of his time in Mexico, setting up loads with Hector. Despite the early reticence of his grandmother, Hector had netted over $2 million in the marijuana trade. That had her full attention. Meanwhile, Richard Nixon devoted his attention to stocking the DEA toolbox with useful implements like no-knock warrants, mandatory sentencing, kingpin statutes, and the liberal approval of wiretaps. Conspiracy laws were strengthened, and budgets increased. The DEA was beginning to find their groove. But still, they operated at a significant disadvantage, having to enfold their case in the nurturing bosom of the Constitution.

The agency knew it was unlikely they would ever catch the likes of Jack and Mike in the act. So they resorted to a strategy of snitches. There were always those more than willing to flip in exchange for reduced time. And if none could be coerced, one or two could certainly be manufactured. It was a self-perpetuating cycle, fueling the engine of a hot new industry called drug enforcement. And if a few pesky amendments had to be overlooked, so be it. The righteousness of the results will always trump the rule of law.

MIKE HALLIDAY

A couple of years after Dave Blott went away, I basically got busted and sent to La Tuna for 900 pounds. It was a product we didn't even want, mostly end-of-season shit— seeds and stems. Not the quality to warrant our A-team to go get it. But Panchelli really wanted to do it. He had a buyer lined up. We could make a little money without having to lift a finger. So I decided to let him and a couple of our guys bring the load across and deliver it to his buyer. Jack didn't want to mess with it. And my only involvement was that I stopped by the stash house to talk to the driver before he left with the load.

The driver got as far as Van Horn before he was pulled over. I barely made it home. They had been watching the stash house. When they saw me walk in, they're thinking, "Jackpot!" I was only there for about ten minutes. But by the time I pulled into my circular driveway, they were already waiting. My son was at the window watching. And they took me away.

I didn't really know Panchelli's buyer—a guy named Rico—one of those guys always hanging around looking for leftovers. I knew who he was, but we had never done business. He was Panchelli's guy. It turns out that Rico got busted a few weeks before, and he's the one that set me up.

It was a bad bust. The feds knew their snitch couldn't testify against me. We'd never been in the same room together. All they had was the ten minutes I spent at the stash house with a load that was busted without probable cause.

Lee said he was going to bypass the jury, let the judge rule, and we'd take our chances on appeal. By the time that happened, the transcripts had been changed to say that the feds had stopped the car for fraudulent plates and smelled the pot. That was bullshit—nothing about fraudulent plates ever came out in the trial.

But that's the way the game is played. So I did every day of my time while Lee Chagra kept pumping sunshine up Jack's ass and spending my money like it was his.

JACK STRICKLIN

Dave was gone. Mike was gone. I lost a truck, a driver and a couple of crew guys—I now had five families to support plus my own. So, on top of everything else, I had to come up with $10,000 a month right off the top—all because of some gutless snitch and a deal we never should have fucked with in the first place. I was pissed off. And I let my emotions get the best of me.

I had never met the snitch—but I knew his name was Rico. I had actually loaned his crew some radios one time, and I never got them back. The other thing I knew about him was that he had a very distinctive four-wheel drive truck—lift kit, huge tires. There wasn't anything like it on the road. He had some serious money in it.

I went to Hector's (an El Paso Café) to eat one morning. I was by myself reading the paper. I looked out in the parking lot, and there was that truck. I looked around the restaurant and noticed three guys sitting at a table. They're laughing and joking, and I'm thinking, "One of those assholes could be the snitch that got Mike, and he owes me some fucking radios on top of it." I went to the phone and called Johnny Milliorn. I said, "Bring Jimmy and come to Hector's now."

If Johnny and Jimmy had shown up one minute later, the whole thing never would have happened. But they showed up exactly when these guys were leaving. So I got up, and we all walked outside. There was three of them and three of us. And I told Johnny and Jimmy, "This guy owes us money. One of them is named Rico, and he owns that truck. I think he's the guy that set up Mike."

And then I said, "If these guys say one fucking thing…"

So they came out, and I said, "Hey, which one of you is Rico?" They all kind of looked at each other and said, "There's no Rico here."

I said, "Nobody here named Rico?"

They said, "No."

"Well, then who the fuck owns that truck?"

He said, "Well, I—" And that's as far as he got.

Jimmy Milliorn coldcocked him. Johnny hits this other guy. And when the guy that was paying the bill comes around the corner, I took him to the ground. I knew immediately the whole thing was a huge mistake. I'm thinking, "Oh man, did you fuck up bad."

Well, the ass kicking's over pretty quick. Street fights don't last long. And now I've made a fool of myself, but I might as well play it out. So I said, "You tell Rico that he's gonna get a lot worse ass-kicking than you just got."

Meanwhile, no one's paying any attention to the guy that Jimmy hit. He's gone to the truck and comes back with a fucking gun. We didn't have guns—we never carried guns. And here I was looking down the barrel of a 9-millimeter, and he said, "Fuck you, man!"

This is how clever I was. I said, "Fuck you" right back.

And he said, "I'm gonna kill you." And he goes: *Boom*! And I could feel the bullet pull my shirt.

I started back towards the restaurant pretty quick, and Johnny reaches out, jerks me in. A tire tool hit that door right after he closed it. We looked in that restaurant—it was totally empty. And Hector, the owner, is yelling at me, "Get out—just get out!"

I said, "What about the check? I haven't paid my check." He just looked at me, and I got the message. We walked out right as the cops blocked the exits to the street.

They were arrested because of the gun. We got to walk away. But those guys had nothing to do with the motherfucker who gave up Mike. One of the guys had just bought a truck from him. I ended up paying their bond, and I had Lee get 'em off—I even replaced the pistol they lost.

SKY HIGH

Mike Halliday

After I got busted, I was in jail for thirteen days before I got out on bond. Lee would have had Jack out in an hour and delayed the trial for two years. But I got busted in November of 1972 and ended up going to La Tuna in early January of '73. I think Lee was happy to see me go. As long as Jack looked after Karen and the kids, I wasn't going to worry about it.

At that moment, it happened to be our busiest time, in the fall. It was also the time we were switching to airplanes full time. The mordida along the border was getting heavy—the Mexican police were greedy. We decided to fly right over the top of it and to hell with the Mexican police.

So I'm awaiting sentence and Jack asks me if I'd go down to Mexico and build a landing strip in Casas Grande. I said, "Jack, I can't go across the border. I'm on bond."

And Jack said, "Mike, here's all you got to do. You go over there, get with Hector, get a crew. Go to this farm in Casas Grande and make an airstrip. We'll come in with two planes, load them up, drop them off, come back, pick you up with the rest of the product, and fly you back to the States."

"Okay, I'll do that."

So I go down there with Hector and Beto, a couple of trucks full of guys and a bunch of shovels and rakes. I'm glad I did because this was one of the most spectacular places I've ever seen in my life—the Sierra Madres in the background. It was beautiful, and the weather was perfect. The only problem was I couldn't get the damn Mexicans to understand they had to rake all the bumps and stuff out of the strip. They just would not fucking pay attention to me.

Finally out of desperation, I got them all in this car, went down to the end of the strip and floored it. Those little bumps were sending the car all over the road. And the guys were like, "Holy shit, what are you trying to do, kill us!"

"Bump, bump, bump," all the way down to the end and I said, "Okay, now listen. Do you see how big these tires are? Those plane tires are much smaller. Do you understand the problem now?"

"Yes, yes, we understand the problem." Man, they smoothed the hell out of that strip.

That night—I don't remember who the pilots were—but one guy had a Cessna 206, and the other guy was flying a Piper with a low wing. So the guys loaded the planes, we put some fuel into them—everything was great. The first plane that took off was the 206. And let's say that the runway we built was a little more than an eighth of a mile. Well, this guy with the 206, he just went about fifty feet and was up in the air and gone. These poor Mexicans that I horrified, they're looking at me like, "You motherfucker. You had us build a quarter-mile runway and you only needed fifty feet!"

I didn't have an answer for that.

So the next plane, which was a low-winged plane, he starts moving down the runway and he goes and goes and goes. We had the car at the end of the runway with the lights blinking on it, so he knew where it ended. And you could just see everybody kind of lifting their hands, like "Get up, get up." And right at the end, "Sky King!" He just barely cleared the car and the fence and off he went. And everybody was like, "Now we know why you wanted it so long."

And then what happened was the weather changed. The pilots never came back. So when we finally realized the weather was coming in, we headed to Juarez. Only now I had no way of getting back into the U.S. It turned out the last time I ever saw Hector and Beto was the night they smuggled me back across the river.

Sometimes we'd bring our loads across by Ascarate Park. So Hector took four of his biggest guys. We had gotten word to Jack so everybody knew what was happening. We had the levee covered with radios. All we needed was two minutes of no Border Patrol. We finally get the word it's all clear, and Hector tells his guys, "Okay, carry him across."

They just looked at Hector and didn't blink an eye. It was a cold night, but those guys got in the river with the water up to their knees, and they grabbed hold of me. It was like how they do crowd surfing at concerts. They walked me across the river and plopped me down on the other side. I walked up on the levee and Jack and Johnny were waiting in the car.

I didn't know it at the time, but I would never see Hector or Beto again. I heard they were both killed in separate car accidents while I was in La Tuna. Smuggling me back to the U.S. was the last river crossing we ever did. After that, I went to prison and Jack went to airplanes full time.

Jack Stricklin

There were two reasons we made the switch from trucks to airplanes. The mordida was one, but the second reason—and the biggest reason—is that the Border Patrol had installed checkpoints at every major road out of town. They had the authority to search any vehicle. We spent a lot of time trying to figure out how to get around them. It couldn't be done without serious risk.

But the thing is, in order for the Border Patrol to operate their checkpoints they had to be within a 100 miles of the border. An airplane could land beyond the checkpoints, no problem. I'd been using airplanes for a while. I actually owned a couple of 206s, kept them at a little airport at Sunland Park. But once the DEA found out about them, we couldn't get off the ground without a police escort.

We had a Mexican who was flying loads out of Chihuahua. He brought us those Christmas-paper bricks everybody loved. He got killed on a landing strip down around Chihuahua. Cows ran out, he pulled back the stick and lost power and stalled. He was carrying 55-gallon barrels of fuel at the time. They didn't ignite, they came forward and cut his head off.

That was about the time Lee Chagra introduced me to Marty Houltin. Marty was a former Air Force pilot. He'd been running shit into Mexico for a few years. And he finally figured out that flying home in an empty plane was a waste of time and fuel. So he got into pot and realized it paid a lot better than sewing machines and cigarettes.

After Lee introduced us, Marty flew me down to Mexico to show me some product, which I wasn't all that impressed with. But what bothered me even more was that our trucks carried a bigger payload. You couldn't put 2,000 pounds in a 206. You could put 800 pounds. And I told him that. I said, "Hell, our truck can carry more than your airplane."

Marty just looked at me and said, "Well Jack, we'll just have to get more airplanes."

They called Marty Houltin the Little Palomino. He was small in stature with a flowing blonde mane and a defiant strut. A legend of the subculture, Marty was the first U.S. pilot to engage federal officials in aerial confrontation.

With a U.S. Customs plane hot on his tail, Marty Houltin landed at a small airport near Las Vegas, Nevada, hung an abrupt U-turn at the end of the runway and accelerated full speed toward the pursuing aircraft. It was a high-stakes game of chicken that ended with Marty lifting off seconds ahead of a disastrous collision. But he bought himself enough time to jettison his load and escape the pursuit of U.S. Customs.

Such is the legend of Marty Houltin, credited with everything from pioneering the aerial smuggle to the invention of cannabis. Where fact and fiction diverge is anyone's guess. The only thing I really know about Marty is that he was never one to discourage the advancement of his own image. If I had to describe his relationship with Jack in a single word, I would say it was competitive.

In 1968, Marty Houltin moved to Columbus, New Mexico, a tiny border town about seventy miles due west of El Paso. From a field of caliche and rock, the Houltins had jokingly christened

L to R: Unknown, Jack Stricklin, Marty Houltin and Jim French of the Columbus Air Force, ca. 1974

Columbus Municipal Airport, Marty smoothed out a landing strip and created a remote hub for a handful of independent contractors who would come to be known as the Columbus Air Force. It was a loosely affiliated group of like-minded ex-military pilots with a taste for easy money and the nerve to land on a mountaintop and bring back a load of pot in the dark of night through a narrow mountain pass, at ten feet off the deck.

Dried-out lakebeds and remote pipeline roads were occasionally employed for landings, but Jack preferred the long, straight highways of Northern New Mexico. They were safer to land on, lightly travelled and sufficiently remote. He employed a landing guy who did nothing but look for appropriate sites. Jack Stricklin never used a location he hadn't personally checked out.

Jack always designated a secondary landing spot in case the primary was compromised. A small crew would be stationed at the backup, usually near a culvert so the pot could be stashed until the rest of the crew arrived with the trailer. Jack had an aptitude for organizing landings. Though Marty Houltin is often credited with the origin of the airplane smuggle, Jack Stricklin was landing planeloads of pot long before Marty ever entered the picture.

The Cessna 206 was Jack's airplane of choice, ideal for short field landings and takeoffs with a capacity of about 800 pounds. Two planes were normally used, so the first pilot could be offloaded while the second watched overhead for approaching vehicles. Once the first plane was unloaded, that pilot would take off and keep watch for the second plane. There were radios, of course. But not a word was ever spoken.

Click. "I'm here".

Click, click. "Bring it in."

From calm to chaos in the blink of an eye, it was a rich mixture of terror and adrenaline as cars raced to light up the highway. Almost out of nowhere, a surprisingly large airplane came down right on top of you, engines whining and tires squealing as it hit the blacktop. The crew moved full speed, typically completing the offload in less than five minutes. Sometimes the planes would need fuel, which meant pumping gasoline from a 55-gallon drum through a T-shirt or strainer. It was a chore usually handled by Johnny Milliorn while the rest of the crew was transferring the pot. On a good night, the landing was orchestrated with the precision of a NASCAR pit crew. It was a beautiful thing when it worked, but there were a lot of moving parts and events could go south in a hurry.

JACK STRICKLIN

I remember one night we were out waiting for a couple of planes—we'd been chasing this load for a few days and it finally came together. It was a perfect night. We get the signal and started moving. I'm in the lead car with Johnny, the offload crew is right behind us, with Billy Russell pulling the trailer.

We chased the plane 'til it came to a stop. As I jumped out of the car, I looked back and saw a set of headlights that weren't supposed to be there. The second pilot has to make sure the area is clear. But just behind Billy comes this fucking semi-truck and he's barreling down on us like a freight train.

So I'm standing there like a dumbshit wondering how the guy got so close, but Billy Russell is all over it. He pulls his car and trailer around and heads straight for the guy. Horns are honking, air brakes are screaming. Billy Russell is about to be flattened by a semi. And we're just standing there staring.

All of a sudden Billy whips that trailer across the road right in the path of the truck. It finally stopped about six feet away. So Billy calmly gets out with his cowboy hat on and walks up to the truck driver with a friendly smile and says, "Sorry for the inconvenience. If you could give us a few minutes, we'll be out of your way."

Turns out the truck driver had pulled off the road to take a nap, and woke up right in the middle of our landing. When I went to talk to the guy, I could tell he knew exactly what we were doing—he was really nervous. But I peeled off about $500, and he drove away with a smile on his face.

I had one of the guys follow him a little way just to make sure. But it could have been a shit storm—I mean, we all stood there like deer in the headlights. But Billy Russell put himself between us and that semi-truck with no hesitation. He really showed me something that night.

The transition to airplanes altered the complexity and economics of Jack Stricklin's operation. Weather and communications were always a problem. The Mexicans wanted more money, the pilots wanted more money, and for the first time, competition was at his heels. Between rival smugglers and the DEA, the game board was becoming cluttered. In fact, one tiny mile marker on an expansive grid of New Mexico state highways was all the proof Jack Stricklin ever needed that his advantage was beginning to erode.

One night, as he and his crew approached a favored landing spot to prepare for the offload of two planes, they ran into a rival crew set up at the exact location awaiting airplanes of their own. Years later, the encounter might have been a cause for violence. But to Jack it was a simple case of running into old friends in unexpected places. He laughed it off and got down to the business of blending the crews and transforming a deserted New Mexico Highway into O'Hare International on Thanksgiving weekend. The planes were put into an orderly holding pattern as, one by one, they ascended to dispatch their loads, take on fuel, and disappear into the pre-dawn sky.

Jack may have been amused by the unexpected encounter, but he didn't fail to get the message. The logistical and mechanical pitfalls of a complicated smuggle, the competition for steady supply, and the escalating tenacity of the DEA meant he would just have to work harder to maintain his edge. Ironically, the man who never again wanted to work on his father's pipeline would be putting in overtime to maintain a pipeline of his own.

Jack Stricklin

Dave had been busted. Mike had been busted. And I was going down to Mexico, loading airplanes, coming back out, landing them, loading the trucks, collecting money, going back to Juarez, into the interior. I wasn't doing any kind of drugs. I got down to 150 pounds because I wasn't sleeping, and I wasn't eating. I was just running. Johnny was driving, and we never stopped. We couldn't. We had to keep the wheels turning. Your suppliers don't care about your problems. If you can't take their weed, somebody else will. So I'm moving product as fast as they can send it. We were doing a minimum of two loads a week. I was working my ass off.

One day I came home and my roommate at the time says, "Jack, some guy by the name of Paul keeps calling and wants to talk to you."

And I said, "I don't know anybody by the name of Paul, and I don't want to talk to him."

Just then the fucking phone rang. I picked it up, and this guy says, "Jack?"

"Yes."

"My name's Paul."

"I don't know you, man."

And he said, "I know you don't. But I'll tell you what you need to do. You need to come meet with me. Let me do the talking. You do the listening."

The last thing I wanted to do was go out and meet somebody I didn't know to talk about shit I didn't want to talk about. What I wanted was a nap. But I go out and drive down to the Waffle House on Mesa Street.

I'm waiting in my car and out walks this guy with a serious limp. He gets in the car, pulls up his pant leg, and said, "That's a bullet wound and it really hurts."

I'm thinking he's going to tell me this great story about

how heroic he was or something because right away, I smell cop. And I said, "What happened?"

He said, "I shot myself."

By now I'm pretty convinced this isn't going to end well, but I said, "Okay, what do you want to talk about?"

He said, "Do you remember when your apartment was bugged, and you found the bug by accident?"

I said, "Yeah."

He said, "I wired that apartment. I'm connected with the Government—I'm not a fed, but I'm connected with them. I do black bag jobs for them."

I'm starting to feel like I'm in a James Bond movie—"The Spy Who Shot Himself." I have no idea where this guy is going. Then he says, "But I'm also connected to an agent who's real strong, very high up. And we want to sell you weed."

"You want to sell me weed?"

"Yeah."

"And exactly where are you getting this weed?"

"It's all confiscated. It's already here. We'll deliver it past the checkpoints, anywhere around Albuquerque you want."

I said, "What's the price?"

"$50 a pound."

I was paying anywhere from a $100 to $150 a pound and I had to pay pilots to get it across the border and past the checkpoint. I asked him, "Is there any way I can get hold of you?"

He said, "No, but I know where you'll be. Did you notice that you hadn't been in your house for five minutes when I called?"

So out of nowhere I've got this nut job offering to supply me with government weed at half of wholesale. I mean if this isn't entrapment, I'll kiss a pig. When I told Lee Chagra about it, he just laughed and said "You can't be entrapped, Jack—entrapment is what they do to innocent people."

I honestly think if I hadn't been so worn out, I would have probably told The Spook to fuck off. But as hard as I was working to scrape a little profit out of every deal, I wasn't sure how much longer I could hang on by myself. So a few days later he calls me and I said, "Let's meet."

We met, and I told him to deliver a load to the Hilton Inn in Albuquerque on Saturday.

"Okay."

"How much are you going to send?"

He said, "Well, let's start off with a thousand pounds."

I said, "Okay, I'll pay you after the load is delivered safely and distributed wherever I decide to send it."

"Fine with me. We don't care where you send it."

I'm still thinking this might not be the smartest thing I've ever done. I said, "Let me ask you something, why did you pick me and my crew?"

He said, "Only one reason."

"What is it?"

"You guys don't talk. We've got files on you. We've got pictures of you and all your crew. We know who you are and what you're doing, and we know that not one member of your crew has ever turned snitch."

So I said, "Okay, see you in Albuquerque."

Johnny Milliorn, Billy Russell, and I drive to Albuquerque, and we can't find the guy. He's just not there. So I go out the back of the hotel to look in the parking lot. Nearly every car out there has got an antenna on it. I told Johnny, "There's something wrong here. Look outside."

He looks out and says, "Jesus, those are all cop cars!"

And I said, "It couldn't be. They're not that stupid. Go walk around and see if you can find out anything."

About ten minutes later, Johnny comes in the room just laughing his ass off. He says, "They're holding a convention next door, and they ran out of parking space for all these cops. It has nothing to do with us."

So we go back downstairs, and there stands The Spook.

"Okay, let's go." Billy Russell follows with the trailer, and we drive to a little shack just outside of Albuquerque. I tell The Spook, "Get out of the car and walk down that road about half a mile. I'll pick you up after we check out this load."

He says okay, and he gets out and limps down the road. Billy, Johnny, and I tore that weed apart. We combed through every bit of it, and we can't find any bugs. The load was clean. So we put it in the trailer and Billy headed for Atlanta. And that's how we got into business with the feds.

We probably ended up doing close to 15,000 pounds with The Spook—at $50 a pound—delivered outside the checkpoint. It was the sweetest deal I ever did. They gave us paperwork for the drivers in case we got stopped. The paperwork said, *This is an official sting operation. We're working such and such. Leave them alone.* It was the only time in my life I ever cooperated with the Government. And I made a lot of money doing it.

PIVOT POINT

On a sunny June morning in 1973, federal agents appeared at Lee Chagra's office with a warrant for his arrest. Lee had been named in a conspiracy that would ensnare over forty people, including Jack Stricklin, Mike Halliday, Johnny Milliorn, and a good portion of their crew. The feds had to be positively giddy to see Lee Chagra in handcuffs on the front page of the afternoon

L to R: Jack Stricklin and Billy Russell, somewhere in the New Mexico desert, ca. 1975

edition of the old *Herald Post*. Johnny Milliorn and several others were arrested with far less fanfare. Like Lee, they quickly made bail. Mike Halliday was already in federal custody and would soon be transferred to Nashville County.

Jack Stricklin was on vacation in Europe when the indictment came down. On Lee's advice, he flew straight to Nashville to turn himself in. Lee would arrange his bail with a local bondsman. But when Jack showed up at the courthouse, no one there seemed to have a clue as to the specific charges. So Jack Stricklin, a prime target of the DEA, was released on his own recognizance. That was the first sign that the case of the Nashville 40 was more a wish list of vague accusations than a serious indictment.

Not that the feds weren't ecstatic to get their hands on Jack Stricklin and Mike Halliday. But it was Lee Chagra who captured most of their attention. They were so convinced he was the man behind the curtain and had invested so much money and manpower trying to prove it, they were prepared to hitch their wagon to a team of cats.

Mike Halliday

It took a while to sort it all out, but between Jack and Lee and me, we eventually got the whole story.

After the indictment came down, I ended up being transferred to the Nashville County Jail—the hardest time I ever did. They tried to get me to turn snitch, and they made sure every day of my life was as miserable as they could make it. I had a very painful abdominal hernia while I was there. The only way I was getting any help was to roll over. Fuck that. I made myself a little stinger to heat some water and came up with my own hot water bottle.

Anyway, it turns out there was a lawyer. I'm not going to mention his name, but he was right in the middle of it. I don't know who the other people involved in the police department were. But it's on the record—they had a scam going. They were busting drug dealers—anybody with money, and they would take them to jail, put them into the interrogation room, and put the fear of God in them.

Tommy Pitts had turned into a junkie by this time. We'd been selling to him and his partner since that first twenty-five pound deal in the desert. But we had to cut him off when he got strung out on heroin.

When the Nashville police picked him up, Tommy Pitts started naming names like he's the Yellow Pages. He's telling them about all the pot we sold him. The cops couldn't take notes fast enough. When Tommy's finally done, they stick all the notes in the drawer and take him to a cell.

By now, he's probably in the early stages of withdrawal. And the cops say, "Tommy, there's an easy way out of this."

"What do I have to do?"

"Just call this attorney—he has an in with the prosecutor. For the right kind of number, this thing can go away forever."

They never intended to prosecute anybody. They didn't give a shit about busting us. They just wanted to rip off Tommy Pitts. He ended up giving them maybe $50,000. But I know he was never fingerprinted, never processed through the Nashville jail, never charged.

What happened next was some cop went and opens this drawer and pulls out this paperwork and starts reading about all these people who have been dealing huge quantities of pot in Nashville. He notices most of the guys were from El Paso, so he figures he better let people there know they were working on a case.

When he called El Paso and mentioned the names Lee Chagra and Jack Stricklin, word got to Judge Ernest T. Guinn pretty fast and he just said, "Arrest them. Go get them right now." He never bothered to look at the evidence—he just saw those names and started foaming at the mouth.

It wasn't until after the arrests were made that

somebody in El Paso finally decides to let the cops in Nashville know they were following up on the case.

They said, "What case?"

"Well, the case you're working on, the guys from El Paso."

"Holy fuck, we're not working on a case in El Paso."

This was a rip-off. This was not a case—it was never a case. The whole thing was just an excuse to fuck with us—all because the feds had such a hard-on for Lee Chagra.

The Nashville case dragged on for close to two years. More than 150 separate motions were filed by the defense, with the Government failing to respond to all but a few. After a full year of back and forth, charges were dropped against more than half of the Nashville 40. But the U.S. attorneys refused to let go of the case against Lee Chagra, Jack Stricklin, and Mike Halliday. By the time all charges were quietly dismissed as a result of the failure to provide a swift and speedy trial, they were nearly broke.

In 1975, Frank Grey Jr., Chief Judge of the Middle District of Tennessee, wrote that the indictment of the Nashville 40 was "…worded as to be utterly meaningless and actually charged the accused with nothing at all." He added that the conduct of the Government violated basic principles of justice. He recommended a thorough investigation into the relationship between a certain Nashville attorney and the Nashville Police Department.

Though the Justice Department failed to try a single member of the Nashville 40, the damage they inflicted was a game-changer. The last thing a drug dealer needs is a lawyer facing a felony indictment for dealing drugs. Lee Chagra's practice didn't totally dry up, but it slowed to a trickle.

For Jack Stricklin, the two-year legal battle was a crippling inconvenience. He continued to work—he had no choice. Legal fees had consumed most of his cash and all the investments he and Mike once held. Families and crew still had to be taken care of, and the pipeline demanded to be fed.

After his profitable dealings with The Spook, Jack found himself once again competing for the best loads. The business of Mexican pot was no longer a cakewalk for cash. The Mexicans were wearing out their dirt, pulling pot out of the ground, and replanting with no regard for the condition of the soil. Loads were slow to sell, and customers were complaining of a product that had become generic. The market was leaning to more exotic strains. And for the first time, Jack Stricklin found himself behind the curve, straddling the line between desperation and hope.

In the summer of 1974, Jack was working on a load that had already fallen victim to weather, mechanical issues, and tangled logistics. But Jack stayed positive—patience is the smuggler's patron saint. At the moment, however, Jack's patience was being tested by the fact that he was in the middle of the Navajo Indian Reservation awaiting the delivery of two planeloads of pot. And he was completely surrounded by the tribal police.

Jack Stricklin

We had an El Paso Natural Gas Company landing field on the Navajo Reservation in Arizona. When we got there, it looked great. There was nobody around. But when we showed up to do the load, the tribal police were everywhere.

We'd been there to look around. We knew the roads. We planned escape routes. We knew all that. But we didn't have any idea that all these people were going to show up—trucks were driving by every five minutes. It was like somebody built a mall out there. Thankfully, there was a storm somewhere between the pilots and us, and they didn't come. If they had shown up, we'd have probably had to wave them off.

So we snuck out of there that night and headed for Roswell, New Mexico. I had heard about a place with a nice little landing strip. We were trying to land two twin engine Beech 18's—about 4,500 pounds. And it sounded like it might work. So I sent one of the guys ahead to check it out.

BILLY RUSSELL

You have to remember that in 1974, communications was nothing but landlines and radios. The phone system in Mexico was primitive at best—you could lose a whole day just trying to get hold of the pilots. Delays were pretty common, but we'd been chasing this particular Mexican load for more than a week, and that's unusual. Traveling that area with a trailer and a couple of trucks full of guys could get noticed in a hurry. So by the time we got to Roswell, everybody was on edge. But the place looked perfect—a long, smooth dirt road in the middle of nowhere.

I had a big 6' by 12' trailer I was pulling with my own car—the Impala. The landing was routine. It came off without a hitch. But we only got half the load, each plane was only half-full. That's the way things were going at the time. But half a load was better than nothing.

As I was driving out with the load, the pickup with all the crew was in front of me. So we're driving along kicking up dust. Through the haze, I see red lights flashing up ahead. I said, "Oh shit," and geared down, opened the window, and threw the keys to the trailer out into the desert. No sense making it easy for them. But I knew we were cooked. There was nowhere to go. Red lights in front of me, red lights behind me, and I was on my way to jail.

Jack Stricklin

I broke my own rule. I deserved what happened to me, but not what happened to everybody else. That was my fault. My rule was never, ever go into a place I hadn't checked out myself And I never checked this place. I got pushed into it because we really needed the load, and we didn't have a place to land it. We were in a hurry. I got careless.

I had no idea it was a game preserve. I mean who in the hell knew game wardens were watching this place for poachers! That's what they thought we were. They didn't stop us for pot—they were looking for dead antelope. There were only three of them, and they had no idea what we were doing. A lot of the guys got away into the desert. But the rest of us were stuck.

When they searched the truck, they found an old .22 magnum that I didn't know was there. There was also a hunting knife. There were a couple of flashlights on the floor. But what really got their attention was the night scope—state of the art. The feds had nothing like it. The game warden was checking it out, asking a lot of questions. The other warden was turning over a bedroll in the back of the truck and found a brick of pot we had opened up to look at. That guy turned around and went *crack, crack* with that shotgun and said, "Nobody move!"

So it was on that early morning of August 18, 1974, that officer Larry Turner, along with officers Tom Moody and Lloyd Haun of the New Mexico Department of Fish and Game, accomplished by accident what the DEA had been attempting since inception. They nailed Jack Stricklin & Company in a solid gold bust. The gun, the flashlights and the night scope were all the probable cause they needed to search the trailer for illegal game. The brick of pot was the final nail. The DEA was called in. Everyone was taken to the Chavez County jail. And Jack Stricklin, Billy Russell, and five members of the crew were looking at the certainty of prison time.

Jack, of course, refused to dwell on it. Nothing could change the events of Roswell. He knew Lee Chagra could delay the trial long enough for him to get back on his feet. Just as he knew that the future of his business now lay in other directions. It was time once again to change the paradigm. Jack didn't yet know how he would do it. But the distant cry of *Colombia* was resonating up and down his pipeline. He knew he would have to answer.

His first order of business, however, was to get everyone the hell out of the Chavez County jail.

JACK STRICKLIN

So there's this big fat white guy in the Chavez County Jail with us. This is the worst jail I've ever been in in my life, and I've been in some really shitty jails. But this one was terrible—the food was horrible, made you sick. It was just filthy, and this big fat boy was in the same tank with us. When it came out on the news that we got busted with 2,200 pounds of marijuana, we became kings of the jail. I mean, "You guys got 2,200 fucking pounds of pot? No shit? You need anything?"

Well, one day I notice this old man on a crutch, and he's walking through the jail, and this fat guy says to me, "See that old man right there?"

"Yeah."

"That's who you want to talk to."

I said, "Who is he?"

He said, "He's a bondsman."

"Oh, I've got my own bondsman, I don't need him."

We stayed in that shithole for another day, and I finally

said, "Bullshit. Get that guy. I want to hire him. I want him to bond us out."

So after a little while the guy's assistant comes up, and the guards immediately open up the gate and call my name, "Mr. Stricklin?"

"Yes."

He puts out his hand, "I'm such and such. We're getting ready to have a little bond hearing for you guys. We understand you're running the show here, so we need you in the hearing."

We go into this magistrate's office. Sitting over against the wall is that old man with the crutch. The magistrate stands up and puts out his hands to shake with me and says, "Mr. Stricklin, they taking care of you boys all right?"

And I said, "Yes sir, we're doing fine. But we'd like to get out."

He said, "Well, we're going to take care of that right now. Looks like everybody's down for $20,000 except for you—seems like they found a stolen pistol."

I had no idea where that pistol came from. I didn't carry guns. I'm pretty sure it was the idiot who directed us to the place. He must have left it in the car when he got away.

"Mr. Stricklin, your bond is $70,000 at ten percent."

I said, "Okay, that's fine."

And then this old man raises an eye and says, "George, I checked on these boys. There ain't no need for a $70,000 bond, and there ain't no need for any $20,000 bond."

Now this is a bondsman. He says, "I think these boys ought to get out on a $10,000 bond each, ten percent, $1,000 apiece. That's what I think."

The magistrate said, "Yes sir, I think you're correct."

Who is this guy?

So they let us out of jail and tell us, "You guys have a nice day now." And as we're walking out the old man says, "Mr. Stricklin, I assume you have the money in El Paso."

I said, "Yes, sir. You're absolutely correct."

"Well, why don't we just take a ride to El Paso?"

"Good idea."

"But you all must be hungry. Let's go grab a little breakfast before we go."

Who is this guy?

Well, we go over to Sambo's, and the old man sits at a table all by himself. Well, I can't take any more of this. So I get up, and I walk over there, and I said, "Can we talk?"

And he said, " Well, of course."

"You just took money out of your pocket. I know what bondsmen get paid, and I know I was willing to pay whatever they asked. I wanted out of jail."

He said, "Mr. Stricklin, I want you to look outside." So I looked out.

"You see all that out there?"

"Yes sir."

"I own it. I own half this town. And you know how I paid for it, Mr. Stricklin?"

I said, "No, sir, I do not."

He said, "The exact same thing you're doing, except I was running whiskey. I was a bootlegger, Mr. Stricklin. I don't need your money, and I like you boys. You remind me of me in my younger days. Those were good times."

PART II
THE NORTH SHORE
1975

LITTLE MISCHIEF

Jimmy Chagra was the second of three brothers—born between Lee and younger brother Joe—who would follow Lee into the practice of law. Jimmy was the classic middle brother, referred to by his family as "Little Mischief." But there was nothing diminutive about the scope of Jimmy's mischief-making. He was a fuckup of gargantuan proportion. He drank, chased women, and, like his brother Lee, gambled to excess. And those were his good points.

Though everything he touched turned to shit, Jimmy always managed a clean getaway, leaving his messes to older brother Lee. Jimmy had married young. His first daughter was on the way when his parents, concerned about his wild ways, mortgaged an investment property and purchased a carpet store for him to manage. They hoped he would at last apply his efforts toward something with a future.

Jimmy applied himself enthusiastically to his new role, appearing in his own commercials and strutting around town like the King of Carpet. He drove a fancy car, wore expensive clothes, and flashy jewelry. He got to be a big shot, just like his brother Lee. Unfortunately, Jimmy's love of the business didn't apply to its day-to-day operation.

Work was to Jimmy Chagra like a treetop to fish. The first sign of trouble may have surfaced when his mother had to call and wake him up for work every day. He managed to mismanage the family carpet store into a death spiral, forcing his parents to seize control of the business and all its assets. Jimmy was just too busy—bowling and shooting pool, high-stakes poker games. If the odds were long enough, Jimmy would bet against death and taxes. He actually managed to beat the taxman for a while, but the reaper remains undefeated.

Jimmy Chagra and second wife Liz, ca. 1975

Like Lee, Jimmy was a compulsive, high-stakes gambler. His trips to Las Vegas with his brother were a daily double of larger-than-life egos inflated enough to believe they could take down a casino—an objective the casinos did everything they could to encourage. Though at the time, Jimmy had nowhere near the resources enjoyed by brother Lee, he had every bit of the nerve. Lee was superstitious, moody, and a horrible loser. Jimmy's gambling was totally without conscience. Never mind if he was down to his last $50 with a wife and child waiting at home. Jimmy would either parlay that $50 into a $1,000 or lose it all. Either way, he was walking out with a smile on his face.

JACK STRICKLIN

> One night, Jimmy beat Don Haskins (head coach of UTEP's 1966 championship basketball team) out of $10,000 playing pool. Jimmy was a pool-shooting motherfucker. He made a fool of Johnny Milliorn. Johnny told me flat out, "That guy is a shark."
>
> The next day I finished working out at the health spa

and I came outside, and Jimmy's sitting there in his Lincoln. So I walked over. "What's up, Jimmy?"

And he said, "I beat Don Haskins out of $10,000 last night, and he wants to get his money back."

"How did you beat him out of $10,000?"

"Playing pool."

"So you're going to play pool again?"

"No, we're going to shoot free throws."

"You're going to shoot free throws with Don Haskins?"

"Yeah."

"I've got to see this."

So we get to the gymnasium at UTEP. This bookie I know is there. I walk in and he says, "Jack, you want some of this action?"

"I sure do, I'll take Haskins."

He said, "No."

"Well, that's who I want. I'm not betting on Jimmy."

"Then there ain't going to be no bet."

So they started shooting free throws. This lasted an hour and a half. Jimmy would shoot ten and make ten in a row. Then Haskins would make ten. Jimmy would make eight, Haskins would make nine. Jimmy would make nine, Haskins would make ten. Jimmy would make five, Haskins would make six. I wanted to say, "Jimmy, haven't you caught on yet?"

After an hour and a half, Jimmy's arm is so sore he can barely lift it. He not only loses the $10,000, he loses $5,000 more. So he pays off, and we said goodbye to Coach Haskins. Jimmy and I get into his Lincoln, and he says, "Oh God, my arm's sore."

I said, "Jimmy, what are you doing the rest of the afternoon?"

And he said, "Well, nothing. Why?"

I said, "Maybe we should go find Mickey Mantle and challenge him to a home-run contest, you fucking moron."

> Jimmy's wife told me I was the only person who talked to him that way. I talked to Jimmy like a dog. Because that's what you had to do sometimes to get through to him.

After nearly bankrupting the family business, Jimmy was liberated to focus all his energy on becoming what he really wanted to be. And what he wanted to be was Lee. Other than himself, the only person Jimmy truly worshipped was his brother. From his larger-than-life persona to his lavish lifestyle, Lee projected exactly what Jimmy wanted to be—rich and respected. Of course, rolling up his sleeves and going to college would be out of the question. Jimmy was the Shortcut Kid. He would find his path to glory without breaking a sweat.

With the colossal failure of his carpet business and the collapse of his marriage, it was only a matter of time before Jimmy Chagra discovered the pot business. He felt his gamblers' temperament was well-suited to running drugs—just as the image of the successful drug dealer was well-suited to his massive ego. It was perfect. He could be just like his brother, without all the hassle of law school.

Jack Stricklin and Jimmy knew each other through Lee. Jack recognized the con man in Jimmy, and, as he was prone to do, overlooked the obvious character flaws. On the plus side of the ledger, Jimmy could be charming, funny, and boldly courageous. He spoke three languages fluently and was a long way from stupid. But when it came to common sense, Jimmy was bereft. He had yet to prove himself as a drug dealer, and Jack wasn't quite ready to welcome him to the fold. But with Mike Halliday away and the business in a slump, Jack observed with curious interest as Jimmy plunged head first into the pot business, without the slightest clue of the water's depth.

Jack Stricklin

My first pot deal was an ounce. Jimmy's first deal was a 1,000 pounds, and he had no idea. He knew somebody who flew a 210 that would carry about a 1,000 pounds. So they landed it up around Vaughn, New Mexico, loaded it in a truck, and Jimmy drove it to Pittsburgh.

So far so good, right? The only problem was Jimmy is driving around with a trailer full of weed, and he has nobody to sell it to. A friend of mine—another smuggler— said to me one time, "You know, Jack, when you and I go off and do a deal, we like to have at least a 50/50 chance of pulling it off. Jimmy will do the deal if his chances are a hundred to one."

Jimmy just didn't care—a one percent chance of success was fine with him. "Okay, let's do it. We've got a shot here."

So Jimmy's driving around with a trailer full of pot in Pennsylvania, and there's this dude just walking down the street. Jimmy pulls over and says, "Hey, man, can I talk to you?"

And the guy says, "Yeah, sure, what's going on?"

Jimmy said, "You smoke pot?"

The guy said, "Yeah."

"You know anybody who would want to buy any?"

He said, "Yeah, me."

And Jimmy said, "Can you buy 1,000 pounds?"

And the guy said, "Let's talk."

And that's where Jimmy got his connect. I think the guy's name was Sammy—whatever it was, Jimmy left him the pot. A couple of weeks later the guy paid him, and he's in business.

The first time Jimmy came to me, he only wanted to deal a few hundred pounds. I said, "Jimmy, really, I don't have time for that." Well, the next time he came to me, he had a couple thousand pounds, but typical Jimmy—he had no way to move it. I didn't have any weed at the time, but I had transportation and buyers. So I said, "How about 50/50?"

He said, "Let's do it." And that's how I hooked up with Jimmy.

Nobody was too happy about bringing him in. But I needed him. Mike Halliday was gone, and somebody had to pick up the slack on that end. I couldn't leave the country. And Jimmy did not shirk, he wasn't afraid. He didn't go hide while everybody went to work. He pulled his weight. He was out there right in the middle of it all. I really think there was something missing in Jimmy's brain. He had no fear, nothing scared him. Nothing. Of course, he didn't have a lick of common sense. I mean, we went into places that I personally wouldn't have gone. But Jimmy just charged straight ahead. I'll tell you what though, he was a producer—he made things happen.

Jack's decision to do business with Jimmy was not a popular one among his crew. To say Jimmy Chagra was a snake would be an insult to snakes. He was totally without loyalty to anyone but himself. He called everyone *Brother*, but given the shit sandwich he kept leaving for his real brother to dine on, no one took much comfort in the word.

To a man, the crew mistrusted Jimmy Chagra. He held to a different set of values and would step on anyone to elevate himself. Jack, on the other hand, was one of the guys—he was first and foremost a trusted friend. Everyone knew if trouble came, he would be there for you. But Jimmy was all about Jimmy. He would kick you to the curb and never look down.

Jack was not blind to the flaws in Jimmy's character. Theirs was a relationship built more on need than trust. But Jack appreciated Jimmy for his nerve and con-artistry. He may have been a lazy smuggler and a sloppy accountant, but Jimmy's ability to bullshit and bully his way to a connection was an asset Jack found hard to resist. He knew if he could talk him into going down to Colombia, Jimmy Chagra would sniff out a connection. So far, that was the sum total of Jack's plan. All he needed to do now was sell it to Jimmy.

THE JACK & JIMMY SHOW

MIKE HALLIDAY

When I went into La Tuna in January of 1973, it was the Jack & Mike show. When I got out in November of 1974, it was the Jack & Jimmy show. I went back to work, but I never saw Hector or Beto again. By the time I got out, I had lost damn near everything—my wife had divorced me and taken the kids. We lost the place in Farmington, the trailer park, the bar. I mean we barely had enough for a six-pack.

On the day I was finally released, Jack and Jimmy picked me up from the county jail and drove me to my parents' house. The first thing I did was change clothes. When I put on my boots, I found $5,000 hidden in one of them. That money ended up going into a hash deal they were doing with one of Jimmy's connects.

It was a guy out of the East Coast named Peter Kruschewski. This is the epitome of how people can be beyond stupid. Peter's people went to Colombia to buy the hash. And the deal was they could buy the lowest quality hash, the blonde hash, which was like $100 a kilo. They could buy the brown hash, which was commercial quality, for $150 a kilo. Or they could buy the black, kick-your-ass hash for $250 a kilo. These dumb-ass motherfuckers bought 4,000 pounds of the $100 shit, and they got it back to the States and couldn't sell it.

We ended up getting rid of it for them, but I don't think we made a dime off the deal. But in the process of moving that Colombian hash, we found out a lot more about how they pulled it off. That hash deal is what put things in motion.

Peter Kruschewski would be an important player in events that unfolded over the next few months. He was a successful dealer from Lansing, Michigan. Like Billy Russell, Peter was a former Army helicopter pilot who had served in Vietnam. In fact, he applied a strict military overlay to his business, building an organization with a vastly different culture than the one created by Jack Stricklin and Mike Halliday.

Jimmy Chagra had met Peter Kruschewski through a mutual friend, Joseph Willmeng—referred to as "Little Joe" by those who knew him. Little Joe had accompanied Kruschewski on a previous buying trip to El Paso, where he met Peter's supplier, Jimmy Chagra. He and Jimmy became fast friends. In fact, Little Joe ended up switching allegiances and moving to El Paso to work for Jimmy on a full-time basis.

When Peter Kruschewski found himself awash in a sea of horrible hash, it was Jimmy Chagra he called to help dispose of it. Jimmy didn't have the infrastructure to absorb that much bad product, but Jack Stricklin had customers who could get it done. Never mind that he lost money in the bargain. Jack was much more interested in the process than the product.

He got to know Peter and learned that he had used a sailboat to bring 4,000 pounds of hash from Colombia to the coast of Massachusetts. The DEA was heavily entrenched in Florida, but they weren't looking that far north. So Peter Kruschewski rented a summer home on the North Shore and employed a small landing crew that was familiar with the waters around Cape Ann. But most importantly to Jack Stricklin, Peter Kruschewski had a connection in Colombia.

Jack Stricklin

Up to now, I was thinking airplanes—that's what I knew how to do. When we started talking to Peter Kruschewski, he tried to sell us on a boat deal—boats, planes—who cares? Somebody needed to go down to Colombia and set it up. I was out on bond, and there was no way I could leave the country. So I said, "Jimmy, don't you understand, this is absolutely perfect for you. You need to go down to Colombia with Peter and put this thing together. You speak Spanish. You're good at what you do. Go do it."

And Jimmy was perfect for it. I mean the guy really was. He had a way with people. You couldn't help at times but like Jimmy. He was funny as shit. And was liable to do anything. I knew he could get it done down there. He said to me, "Jack, what about the loads we're doing up here?"

"What do you mean about the loads we're doing up here? They're half yours and half mine. I'll do the loads. You go to Colombia. When you come back, I'll give you your money."

If I were the one who went down there, Jimmy probably would have stolen as much as he could steal. But he knew I'd give him an honest count, so he agreed to go to Colombia.

In early March of 1975, Peter Kruschewski and Jimmy Chagra met at the Coconut Grove in Miami, Florida, in preparation for a trip to Barranquilla, Colombia. They had agreed to be partners in the venture, with the proceeds split equally between Peter Kruschewski, Jack Stricklin, and Jimmy Chagra. Mike Halliday would get half of Jack's share.

Accompanying Peter was a man named Scott Emlong. Just as

Jack had a fascination with tough guys, Peter leaned toward mass. Scott was a former semi-pro football player turned body builder. Standing a perfectly sculpted 6' 4", he was a man even other men could not fail to notice—a pretty boy but for his size. Though his job was to appear menacing, he didn't really have the acting skills to bring it off. Scott was as easy-going and affable as a labrador retriever—as unlikely to kick someone's ass as he was to begin his day with a donut. You didn't put a body like that in harm's way.

Up until then, the thinking had been that an air smuggle would be the way to go. It was something Jack knew well and was totally comfortable with. But Peter's recent hash deal and an earlier Colombian smuggle had involved a sailboat. He had access to people who could carry up to 4,000 pounds, and he already had experience with a North Shore landing. Jimmy was warming to the idea, but the dynamic between him and Peter was more competitive than cooperative. Like two dogs pissing on the same stump, they jockeyed constantly over the question of leadership.

Jimmy and Peter—along with Little Joe and Scott Emlong—flew to Barranquilla and checked into the El Prado Hotel. They had a little bit of cash, a lot of hope, and only the faintest idea where to begin the search. Peter's former connection was a man named Herrardo who supposedly lived in the area. All they could do was ask around and hope to run into someone who could point them in the right direction. As it turns out, that someone was driving the taxi they just happened to occupy.

As they were driving around, the cabbie seemed to recognize Peter. With Jimmy acting as translator, they struck up a conversation. The driver reminded Peter that they had met on a previous trip. Peter remembered him and inquired about Herrardo. The cab driver told them Herrardo could likely be found in Santa Marta and offered to drive them. So on the following day, the group checked out of their hotel, and the cabbie-turned-connection drove them to the seaside city of Santa Marta, about ninety miles east as the crow flies.

Jack Stricklin

They found Peter's connection in Santa Marta, but Jimmy didn't like him. He was too far from the source, and Jimmy wasn't interested in 3,000 or 4,000 pounds. I also think Jimmy got fed up with Peter's shit. He was probably thinking to himself, "I'm in Colombia. How hard can it be to buy some pot—lots of pot." The Colombians had it and they sure as hell weren't smoking it all. They had to be looking for buyers.

So Jimmy did what he always did. He met a shoeshine boy and turned him into a multi-millionaire. That shoeshine boy turned out to be the nephew of a guy who ran one of the early cartels. Well, Jimmy went through those guys in Colombia like shit through a goose. I mean he spoke perfect Spanish. He spoke Arabic, he spoke English, and he was a con.

It took him about a day and a half to finally connect with a guy named Leonel Gomez. It was love at first sight—Jimmy found a guy who could get his hands on a boatload of pot. And the guy found a crazy American who said, "Give me all you've got." I'm sure Jimmy had him convinced he was the King Kong of the weed business.

That was it. Jimmy gave him what little earnest money he and Jack had scraped together and told him he'd be back in the summer with a down payment. Where that was coming from he hadn't a clue. In fact, he had no idea whether Leonel Gomez could actually come up with a load and a boat to carry it. But in typical Jimmy Chagra fashion, he relied on a gambler's faith and cast the dice with a man he had known for less than forty-eight hours.

JUMPING THE SHARK

The beauty of being a kid is that you can adapt to anything. After living in two different countries and three different states by the time I was ten, I knew how to fit in. I made good friends. As I grew up under El Paso's perpetually sunny skies, I discovered an infinite playground for dirt bikes and dune surfing, four-wheeling, mountain climbing, or just hanging out drinking beer by the river.

We lived most of our life outdoors. When it got too hot, the lake at Elephant Butte Dam was a short drive away. The high mountains were near enough for a day-trip to the ski slopes of Ruidoso in winter or a campout in the uniquely spectacular Gila Wilderness in the summer. There were parties at the river, dances at the YMCA, and cruising on the streets. But what made El Paso such a unique place to grow up was the constant temptation of the border.

Like most people who lived there in the '70s, I developed a keen fondness for the excessive girth of its underbelly and the many fine opportunities it afforded. I don't know what other kids my age were going through, but it's hard to imagine what it must be like to grow up without a border.

Following high school, I was in and out of UTEP like the Mini-Mart, helping myself to a draft-deferment and whatever courses tickled my fancy. It was a strategy that led to quite a few college credits but little progress towards an actual degree. By the end of 1969, the music stopped, and I was left standing on the outside of academic deferment. It had taken me a good three years to finally and irrevocably flunk out.

After being reclassified 1-A, passing my physical and avoiding my mailbox like the plague, I was on a first-name basis with the Navy recruiter and just days away from signing on the dotted line. When the Nixon Administration announced the inaugural draft lottery to be held in December of 1969, I decided to tap the brakes on enlistment and test my luck. I wouldn't have been happy to find myself operating a mop in the middle of an ocean after winning the lottery.

When my birthday was pulled from the drum in the 296th position, it looked like Ho Chi Minh would have to invade Hollywood before I got a call-up letter. So I hung up on the Navy and headed to Europe with a couple of buddies, where I spent the next few months bumming around ancient places, refining my taste for good beer, and finding a bit of the self-confidence to which I had thus far only pretended. I came back to El Paso determined to support myself. And with the help of roommates, brown rice, and the occasional pot deal, I managed to survive.

After several years of turning shitty jobs into less shitty jobs, I stumbled into advertising in 1973. At a previous stop, I had written a monthly column for what amounted to an in-house newsletter. As a result, I was invited to write (strictly pro bono) for an underground weekly newspaper. I put it all together in what masqueraded as a portfolio and made the rounds of local advertising agencies. It turned out there was a demand for English majors after all! I was hired as a copywriter by a small ad agency with a roster of car dealers, a local boot company, a funeral home, and a large bank, among others.

The job of an advertising agency is to spread manure as liberally as the budget allows. In those days, the manure was largely unregulated and particularly pungent. My job was to make it smell good. One of the first big projects I tackled was a catalog for a company called Helen of Troy. They sold wigs. I was tasked with the artful crafting of an engaging paragraph of copy about each and every one of the dozens of different styles and colors in the line. And each had to be distinctly different. I quickly worked my way through *bouncy, perky, exuberant,* and *windswept,* hitting the wall somewhere between *saucy* and *sophisticated.*

After forty-years as an advertising copywriter, my wig catalog remains the epic achievement of my career. I somehow managed to squeeze out enough adjectives to endow every Helen of Troy wig in existence with the unique and fashionable promise of eternally happy hair. My boss was impressed, our client was ecstatic, and I had discovered a talent for the business of bullshit.

I enjoyed a couple of interesting years at the little ad agency. But when they decided to add accounts by merging with a smaller local shop owned by a man who was also a copywriter, I knew my days were numbered. No matter how you looked at it, there was one writer too many. Layoffs in advertising are about as a common as flies in the paddock. But when it happens to you...

In the spring of 1975, it was apparent that something big was in the works. After the Roswell bust, there had been whispered conversations about a possible Colombian deal. Jack and I had discussed it in general terms. He let me know he could use all the help he could get.

Until now I had always been that horse in the steeplechase going balls-out toward the approaching jump, only to stop at the last second and propel its rider the rest of the way solo. But the part of me that wanted to do what Jack did was gaining ground on the part of me that didn't. I was single, twenty-six years old, nearly broke and unemployed. This time I jumped.

At first, Jack pretty much gave me to Johnny Milliorn. Johnny had become so proficient at landing airplanes, Jack could devote his energy to the Colombian deal. On my first landing, I rode with Johnny and a fifty-gallon drum of aviation fuel tied down in the bed of an El Camino. A second car carried two more crew. A third pulled the trailer that would deliver the load. We drove to a remote area of northern New Mexico where the roads were as straight as the widely scattered population. And there we would wait. Waiting, I would quickly learn, was a bigger part of smuggling than smuggling itself.

On this particular night, Johnny and I beheld a spectacular high-desert light show, sipped coffee from a thermos, and waited for an airplane that would never come. There were a million things that could go wrong. And there was no way to let anyone know.

Once the sun started coming up, we knew our night's work was a goose egg, so we headed back to El Paso, stopping off at a little café in Deming, New Mexico for breakfast. It was during this stop with Johnny and the crew that I began to get a fix on what was really going on.

Mexican pot was getting harder to sell. The fields were played out. What had once been a generous money machine was beginning to resemble a stingy slot machine. Between the losses and the legal fees, Jack was nearly broke. Colombian was now the Holy Grail and there was talk of going down there to fill up a DC-3 and land it somewhere in Oklahoma.

"That's not what I heard. Jack wants to bring it in with a sailboat somewhere off the coast of Florida."

"No, it's going to be way too much for a sailboat. I heard we're going to take a boat to Mexico and use our pilots to bring it across."

Stand by to stand by. About the only thing everybody agreed on was that Jimmy Chagra was a snake, Jack Stricklin would find a way to pull a Colombian deal out of his ass, and carrying fifty gallons of aviation fuel in the back of an El Camino was a good way to die stupid.

GROUNDWORK

While my first attempt at an airplane smuggle ended in frustration, my second was more eventful. It was a clear spring night on a starlit road in northern New Mexico when Marty Houltin came roaring out of the darkness and onto the remote highway. I couldn't have been more afraid if I was facing a firing squad.

We would get only one planeload that night. But it would be a planeload to remember. Once the wheels were set in motion, the adrenaline kicked in and fear turned to focus as I worked desperately for the sole purpose of getting the fuck out of there. We emptied that plane and filled the trailer while Johnny Milliorn saw to the refueling. Then we got back in the truck to light up the highway as Marty Houltin positioned himself for takeoff.

Unfortunately, one of the doors on his airplane had not properly closed, interfering with the movement of his flaps. The takeoff became a skidding slalom, ending up by the side of the road with a busted landing gear and a bent wing. Marty seemed to have suffered no ill effects.

As we pulled up, he was calmly talking on the radio. "Mayday. Mayday. This is N-549-Charlie. I have lost power just north of Magdalena over highway six-zero. I'm going to have to put it down somewhere pretty quick." He looked at us and said, "You'd better get out of here. I'll handle this."

Though I later learned it was a load Jack would be lucky to sell for cost, I viewed my maiden voyage as a great success. I didn't run, hide, or cry. And I experienced the adrenaline afterglow of a seismic rush. After that, I started spending more and more time with Jack. He enjoyed hanging out with me, and he loved hearing me tell the tale of Marty Houltin ending up in a heap by the side of the road. It got a laugh every time.

I was never fully paid for my effort. But I received a first-class education at the feet of a master. I had hardly been in the business for a month, and I had already learned that executing a Colombian smuggle when you're as broke as the Ten Commandments is a titanic leap of faith, even for someone as self-assured as Jack Stricklin.

Eighteen months prior, he could have raised the money in a week. Now he would be lucky if he managed to feed the crew. But Jack remained positive, spending his days reassuring his buyers and occupying the demilitarized zone between Mike Halliday and Jimmy Chagra. Mike didn't like Jimmy. Mike didn't trust Jimmy. Mike didn't want anything to do with Jimmy. Other than that, Mike was happy to go along with whatever Jack decided.

Jack decided that Mike was probably right, but given the circumstances, what choice did he have? He, Billy Russell, and a lot of the crew were going to prison—it was just a matter of how long Lee Chagra could delay their trial. Families would have to be taken care of, not the least of which was Jack's own. His wife Donna had just given birth to a baby boy. Jack wasn't going anywhere without making sure there were Pampers in the nursery and cash in the safe.

The truth was that Jack needed Jimmy Chagra. He might not trust him, but he knew there wouldn't be any kind of Colombian deal without him, just as he knew the raising of the money would ultimately fall on his shoulders alone.

It would require Jack Stricklin's greatest asset to generate enough cash to do the job. So he went to work, leveraging the one thing he had in abundance—a widespread and diverse collection of friends and associates. He began with his customers, offering a three-to-one return in product. Over the next several months,

Jack solicited investments from everyone he knew. Invest a $100, get $300 back when the deal is done, or your original $100 back if it doesn't go down. Those were his terms. He backed every dollar with his personal money-back guarantee. As far as the people who knew Jack Stricklin were concerned, that was collateral enough.

JACK STRICKLIN

> After Jimmy made the deal in Colombia, we borrowed $385,000 at three-to-one. Out of that $385,000, do you know how much Jimmy raised?
>
> $20,000. I borrowed the rest of it.
>
> I said to Jimmy, "You do realize that if things go wrong, we have promised half of El Paso that they'll at least get their investment back."
>
> And Jimmy said, "If things go wrong, we're never coming back to El Paso."
>
> Typical fucking Jimmy—he really made me feel warm all over. And Peter Kruschewski didn't put up shit. He was in the deal because he's the one that found the original guy in Colombia. And he was the one that took us to Boston.
>
> The Colombians wanted $250,000 up front. It was going to take every penny of the rest to set things up in Boston. We needed boats. We needed offload houses on the water—vehicles. We had to get everybody there—we had to house 'em, feed 'em. It wasn't going to be cheap.
>
> You know that old saying: an Army moves on its stomach. That's bullshit. An Army moves on its wallet.

When Jack Stricklin says he simply borrowed $385,000 at three-to-one, he's vastly understating the scope of his accomplishment. What Jack did was employ a level of persuasion worthy of the great P.T. Barnum. Businessmen, politicians, friends, family, restaurateurs, old girlfriends, housewives, bartenders, barbers, bondsmen, attorneys—you name it. Anyone with a piggy bank would be offered the chance to triple their money within a matter of months.

I enjoyed a front-row seat to a roadside revival that would heal the sick and raise the dead. Jack the salesman was a phenomenon that defied resistance. People couldn't wait to hand him what in some cases was their life savings. When I think about the way business is done today and remember what Jack accomplished in 1975, I believe he may actually have invented crowdsourcing.

That he could raise so much money in such a short time was a remarkable accomplishment. Nobody asked questions, and nobody questioned his commitment to repay—one way or another. They all knew in general terms what Jack was planning to do with the money and had no problem being part of it. It was almost as if the entire city of El Paso had become stockholders in a publicly traded smuggling enterprise.

Along with his fundraising efforts, Jack met with Jimmy once a day to keep up with the latest developments in Colombia. I knew only that Jimmy was becoming phone pals with someone who was putting together a big load. Once-a-week conversations became twice-a-week conversations. Though many of them were held out of earshot, I gleaned bits and pieces. I knew the deal was going to happen in the Boston area. There would be boats involved. I knew Jack was targeting mid-summer—the high season on Boston's North Shore. The size of the load remained unknown. But I sensed the pressure beginning to build as we approached the ides of May.

For Jack, there wasn't a lot of time to worry. He knew once the boat was in the water, it would be his show to run. He had full confidence in Mike Halliday and the crew. He had the distribution network to handle the tonnage and the infrastructure to store it. But the deal put a whole new premium on peril. Boats instead of airplanes, densely populated coastline instead of remote desert roads, and a traffic-jam of nosey Yankees forever at your bumper.

At the moment, Jack's biggest concern was finding someone to send to Colombia to supervise the load and return with it on the boat. He knew it was a huge job. This was no midnight rendezvous on a desolate highway. This was four to eight weeks embedded in a culture where dollars were gold and human lives a lesser form of currency. Putting oneself willingly into the role Jack had in mind was a nosedive into the unknown, the uncertain, and the unsafe. Send the wrong guy and the whole deal could end up at the bottom of the sea.

Ralph Armendariz was a homeboy, fluent in both English and Spanish. Unlike the muscled up Scott Emlong, Ralph's body was a good deal more functional. He had been an athlete all his life and carried himself with confident grace. He had the bearing of an ex-Marine and the disposition of a man with zero tolerance for bullshit. Play it straight up with Ralph, and you'll have a friend. Play it any other way, and you'll have a problem.

Jack Stricklin had met Ralph through his wife, Donna. She and Ralph had gone to high school together and remained friends. In fact, Donna lived with Ralph and his wife for a short time before she and Jack were married.

Always in search of a strong back and a kindred spirit, Jack recruited Ralph for a few airplane landings and some crosscountry deliveries. Ralph didn't work full time, but he worked enough that Jack recognized in him a valuable combination of street smarts and toughness.

Of course, Ralph Armendariz couldn't sail a boat in a bathtub, and he didn't know starboard from a rusty scupper. But he had a boatload of confidence and was always up for a challenge. When Jack offered him the chance to go to Colombia and shepherd the load to Boston, Ralph understood that he would be on his own down there. There would be no backup on land or sea. It would be totally up to him to make sure the Colombians held up their end of the deal.

TEJANO

Ralph Armendariz was raised in a traditional working-class Latino family. His father was a union man who did a tough and dirty job in order to provide a comfortable home for his family. He presided over his son with unyielding discipline and a healthy measure of machismo.

"If you're going to be a man, you better be able to take care of yourself."

But Ralph was not a man—not yet. He was

First Communion for Ralph Armendariz (center) at El Paso's St. Patrick's Church

just one of the homeys spending every free minute on the vacant lot next door. It was Yankee Stadium and the Olympic Coliseum all rolled into one rock-infested patch of scorched caliche. But it was arena enough for the epic ballgames that ensued daily.

Though Ralph played at a level few of his friends could match, he attended his studies with considerably less devotion. School never quite managed to get a grip on his imagination.

But he was smart enough to keep up with the pack, exerting the minimum effort to ensure his advancement and the right to remain breathing.

"If you're an average student, that's fine," he was told by his father. "But you will not fail—that is not allowed."

From his mother, Ralph received the kinder angels of his nature. He was taught manners and respect, obedience and loyalty. His mother insisted the family attend church together every Sunday, to be followed by lunch at a local restaurant. It was an uninterrupted ritual that would anchor the family through turbulent times.

By the second grade, Ralph's mother was convinced he required the guiding hand of the Catholic Church. He was enrolled at St. Pius, where he would attend through the eighth grade. Never a distraction or behavior problem, Ralph was a go-along kid who quickly learned how to navigate the halls of parochial education. He kept his head down and toed the rigid line inscribed by the nuns who saw to his body, mind, and spirit.

Ralph may not have been an inspired student, but he distinguished himself at St. Pius as an altar boy. He served with pride and devotion. He was well-liked by friends and faculty and buoyantly gifted in all things athletic. He had strength, speed, and coordination. And he loved to compete.

Respect for authority is a fragile thing in a young man's psyche. About the time you discover a crack in your voice and a hair on your chin, you begin to wonder why the people who are enforcing the rules seem to be the people who are breaking them the loudest.

Ralph's faith in God was unshakeable. As an altar boy, though, he was allowed to peek behind the pulpit and behold the frailties of a clergy that was all too human. He got his first glimpse of homosexuality and his first hint of the Holy Roman hypocrisy. It was beginning to occur to him that he was going to have to find his own truth.

Ralph's father viewed it as a sacred obligation to toughen his son with constant criticism. Boys were the gold standard in the

'60s. And their transformation into manhood was a source of deep pride to their fathers. Ralph's father didn't care whether or not his son had a happy childhood. The friction of a whetstone was the only way to hone the instincts of survival.

As he was headed into high school, Ralph staged his first minor rebellion, insisting he be allowed to forego Catholic school and enroll in the public school just across the street. He hardly knew anyone there but thought it would be nice to spend some time around girls. And he knew the athletic program was far better than that of the all-boy parochial schools.

In Texas, high school athletics means football. Ralph played linebacker for El Paso's Burgess High School. But what truly inspired him was track and field. He took up the pole vault and after endless hours of painful trial and error, managed to launch himself high enough to attract notice at meets around the state. Despite a lackluster academic record, Texas Western College (UTEP) came calling. Ralph Armendariz became an NCAA scholarship athlete. Even his father was impressed.

The life of a college athlete is a simple one. Train hard and keep the performance bar moving up, and your academic bar will be placed a little closer to the ground. You take jock courses, receive jock tutoring, and benefit from a jock-friendly grading system. There was an understanding that if you successfully represented the University and made a token effort at your studies, your eligibility would be protected. Unfortunately, Ralph crossed paths with an economics professor who failed to get the memo.

Despite a heroic last-minute effort, Ralph failed his economics class. He and his coaches pleaded for a D, but the professor wouldn't budge. Ralph lost his scholarship. Uncle Sam stood by with open arms.

Instead of getting drafted, what I decided to do was join the Marine Corps Reserves. I had been told by others it wasn't a good choice. But I figured it was the best route for me. All I heard was that it was the most difficult boot camp of all the services, and if you're going to be in a war, you would want to be beside a Marine. So it was a challenge I wanted to take on. Obviously, a few weeks into it, I thought to myself, "Wow, this really might have been the wrong route to go." But I stuck with it.

When I arrived in San Diego, I was presented immediately with the ideology of total humiliation—breaking you down and then bringing you back up with their own ideology, forming the mindset of a killer.

After my second week there, I was called into my drill instructor's office. He proceeded to ask me if I thought I could kick his ass. Knowing it was better not to challenge him, I responded, "Drill sergeant, the private would do everything in his power to protect himself."

My drill instructor responded by saying, "That's not what I asked you. I asked you, do you think you could kick my ass!" I knew that whatever answer I gave was going to be the wrong answer, so I continued to respond by saying, "The private would do everything in his power to protect himself."

So the guy threw me in a wall locker and started beating it with his stick. He kept me in there for a long time. When he finally opened the door, I just fell out onto the floor. I got myself up. As I was exiting the Quonset hut, he was still kicking my ass. A couple of days after that, he made me the squad leader.

I don't know if that was a defining moment in my life. But it was the moment I began to feel confident of my particular abilities of leadership. I paid for every one of my platoon member's mistakes. And I learned that when you come to a place where you're thinking, "That's it. That's as far as I can go," you can go much further. The Marine Corps taught me that. And they taught me if I ever went to war, I would want a Marine at my side.

When I got my first leave, I flew home in my dress blues. I was feeling pretty good about myself. On the second morning, three or four friends came by and picked me up and said, "Let's go spend the day together."

That was my introduction to marijuana.

We spent the day driving around El Paso visiting other people and laughing about everything that we talked about. It was an all-around fun day. I ended up smoking pot with those guys a couple of times while I was on leave. Every time, I liked it more and more. It really made me look at the world around me in a different way. In the '70s, the world around me was a pretty fucked-up place.

After completing six months active duty in the Marine Corps, Ralph returned home, carrying six feet of confidence and thirty pounds of new muscle. He landed an entry-level job at El Paso Natural Gas, a clear path to a career that would have provided him with a comfortable future.

The man returned by the Marine Corps was a different man than the one they double-timed off the bus in San Diego six months earlier. They had grilled him to the toughness of a $2 T-bone. But while the Corps may have fine-tuned his body and spirit, it was pot that awakened his mind.

The consciousness of a generation was expanding in the billowing throes of the demon weed—thinking had become cool. The war in Vietnam was not cool. Racial inequality was not moral. A corrupt government was not acceptable. And pot was

Ralph Armendariz USMC, 1966

not a dangerous narcotic. Why trust a government that couldn't obey its own laws to come up with new ones? And more importantly to Ralph Armendariz, why deliver a basket of mail from one desk to the next when the world is changing before your eyes?

Ralph quit his job and moved to L.A. where he handed out the "Free Press" on Sunset Boulevard. He wandered up to San Francisco and the psychedelic scene of the Haight. And he crossed the Bay Bridge to Berkeley, the Disneyland of civil disobedience. After an eye opening few months on the West Coast, he came home, his ears still ringing with the echoes of righteous indignation. By 1975, marijuana had evolved from a cultural phenomenon to a political cause. And Ralph Armendariz was committed to the crusade.

Ralph Armendariz

> After I got back from the West Coast, I was living in an apartment complex on Rio Grande Street. I got to know the landlord there. He had a connection in Juarez that would bring over marijuana in one-pound bags and stash it in our basement. Sometimes he'd bring two or three hundred pounds. I helped him out now and then and sold to some customers of my own—nothing huge, but I made some pretty good money. At that time in El Paso, it seemed like everybody was dealing pot at one level or another. But what I actually got busted for, I had nothing to do with.
>
> My apartment was on the third floor. I had a neighbor I

got to know pretty well. He had gone out one night to some bar and met an individual who had weapons he was trying to sell. One of them was a machine gun of some type. Anyway, I knew he had them in his place. He showed them to me.

Not too long after that, I left the apartment one day and I noticed there was a Camaro parked across the street with a guy sitting in it reading a book. I had gone to the drugstore and when I returned, he was still there. And that's when I became suspicious. I thought he was there to bust the landlord. So I went to everyone in the building I knew to be holding and told them, "Trouble is coming. Get ready."

And then I went upstairs and told my neighbor. As we were standing at his window facing the street and looking out towards this car, all of a sudden about six or seven more cars came very fast and more or less blocked Rio Grande Street. I saw these people jumping out of their cars and running toward the building, so I immediately ran through my apartment to a little back porch that had a stairway going down to the ground. Then I pushed the gate open to the alley and started to run.

Next thing I heard was a guy yelling, "Stop!" As I turned and looked, he had his pistol up in a two-hand grip. I decided to come to a quick stop. So they came and got me, and they threw me up against a wall. I had a Marlboro box in my windbreaker. Inside it they found about half a joint.

It so happened that the guns Richard bought at that bar were stolen. That's what got the cops' attention. I stayed about ten days in jail on that particular deal. There was something on the radio every fifteen minutes about us being big-time gunrunners—they enhanced it really big. As it turned out on my end, all charges were dropped. I wasn't involved with it. There were no guns in my apartment. I didn't know anything about it.

When something like that happens to you, there's two ways it can go. One is that you're scared straight. The other is that you're pissed off. The government didn't want me smoking pot, but I didn't want to stop. I wasn't afraid of going to jail. I didn't stop smoking, and I didn't stop dealing. I just got a little more careful about it.

It was never a full-time deal for me in those days—a little on the side every now and then, mostly to pay for my own stash. About a year or so after I got back from the West Coast, I got married and joined the union—the same one my father was in. But the work wasn't too steady in those days. So that was about the time I started doing deals with Jack Stricklin. I landed some airplanes and drove some loads. The money was good, but I liked the excitement even better. You get pretty high when you do something like that—pretty high.

When Jack came to me about going down to Colombia, I was a little surprised. I had no idea he was putting together that kind of deal. But going to Colombia and coming back on the boat with the pot—I couldn't pass it up. It was the kind of challenge I welcomed. Of course, I had no idea how fucking hard it was going to be.

THE COLOMBIAN SHUFFLE

In 1975, America was a nation of landlines. A simple phone call to South America could take on the complexities of a nuclear summit. The usual payphones wouldn't do. Jack Stricklin and Jimmy Chagra rented a cheap apartment that was little more than an upholstered phone booth with a TV and toilet.

As if coordinating the calls wasn't complicated enough, completing them required the devotion of a monk. Often, they had to wait for an international operator to call back after securing a line. It could take hours, and the connection would be of such poor quality you had to scream to be heard. The DEA had no need to tap the phones. If they stood within a block or two, they could probably hear the call just fine.

The basis of Jimmy's confidence in Leonel Gomez was his usual combination of blind faith and reckless courage. In Jimmy's world, confident was just another word for clueless. He didn't know Gomez. He didn't know anyone who had ever dealt with him. He could just as easily be dispatching $250,000 into the waiting arms of a psychopath as buying a boatload of pot. The Colombians would happily kill you for a whole lot less. But Jimmy dealt pot like he gambled—without conscience or regret. Fortunately for everyone involved, he seemed to be riding a hot streak. With every call it was becoming a little more apparent that Leonel Gomez might actually have pot to sell and a boat to deliver it in.

Jack Stricklin, who had borrowed nearly every dime of the down payment, wasn't about to hand his $250,000 over to Jimmy

Chagra and wave goodbye. It wasn't as if he didn't trust Jimmy. It was more a case of knowing exactly *how far* he could trust him. And South America was a bit too far. Jack Stricklin, Jimmy Chagra, and Peter Kruschewski ultimately agreed that Little Joe, Scott Emlong and Ralph Armendariz should carry the money to Colombia. It offered a system of checks and balances that was acceptable to all three interests. Once the money was in place, Jimmy and Peter would fly to Colombia, verify the existence of both the load and the boat, and hand over the down payment.

Ralph Armendariz

Jack called and told me the plan was to fly to Miami, take some cash with me, and meet up with two individuals over there. But I had to get a passport, and I didn't have a birth certificate. There was a reason for that—because my dad wasn't my biological dad. And my mom didn't tell me until I was twenty-four years old. And this happened when I was twenty-seven, so I didn't really have a birth certificate, but I had a baptismal certificate. Believe it or not, in Miami, they gave me a passport with a baptismal certificate.

When I flew down there, I was carrying about $80,000 in manila envelopes stacked in a briefcase. In those days you didn't have to go through much security. So I get to Miami, and I meet up with Little Joe and Scott. We had a room together at the Coconut Grove. They had money also. I think we had a total of about $250,000. We probably stayed in Miami three or four days. We took turns going out now and then, but there was always somebody in the room watching the money. When we finally got word to fly to Colombia, we all wore suits and ties. I wore my boots, so I could put some of the money there. We were at the Miami airport in the men's room in three different stalls. The three of us were passing money underneath. We used Ace bandages to hold it in place.

On the plane, we sat in different rows. We didn't know each other. We never talked to each other. When we landed in Barranquilla, we had to go down the steps and walk the tarmac. As soon as you went in the terminal, they started going through your baggage. I was just trying to make sure they weren't patting down anybody, and they weren't.

We had to meet a guy we only knew by the color of his clothing—a green striped shirt. Antonio was his name. He worked for Leonel Gomez, and I got to know him pretty well. We all ended up in his car and drove towards Santa Marta, which was about ninety miles away.

Antonio was driving down the middle of the highway, hauling ass—playing chicken with the other drivers. They don't move until they get close. I'm riding in the back, thinking, "Holy shit, man, you better slow your ass down." But Antonio never slowed down. At one point, he hit a rabbit. Then he slammed on the brakes, went and picked it up, and threw it in the trunk for dinner.

So we get to the Puerto Galleon Hotel. We never had to check in, we just drove back to one of the cabanas on the side. The Puerto Galleon was a very nice place with a huge swimming pool. And right above the swimming pool it had an old wooden boat. The hull of the boat was part of the restaurant. As you walk down to the pool, they had some grills over here to the right, and they would put shrimp on there and lobster and stuff, and you could just pick and eat during the day. And you could walk down these steps to the beach. About half way down the steps you'd take a left, and there was a bar. It was a hell of a place. I never even saw the front desk. But I did know this: I know there were Colombians all around there watching the money. And we never left the money alone.

We stayed there for two or three days, more or less just eating and hanging out. When the Colombians finally came and got us, I was a little leery about it but Little Joe and Scott were there, and we all three kind of hung together. We didn't really trust the Colombians. The cash was always the issue. And that kind of cash could get you killed in no time.

When we left the Puerto Galleon, we traveled maybe twenty or thirty miles, then took a left off the highway into an area that was thick with foliage. It was a bumpy, narrow road that seemed to be headed toward the ocean. It was a totally secluded area—nothing around until we came to this little clearing and a small motel. It was about a hundred yards from the beach and hidden from view in all directions. It was a quiet place. We never saw the Colombians, but we knew they were all around. We also knew that if they were going to kill us and take the money, this would be the place to do it. We weren't paranoid, we were just careful.

We hung there for another two days before we got the call from Jimmy. He and Peter were on their way to Colombia. We were going to meet up in Cartagena.

That next morning, after recounting and repackaging the money, they split up into two taxies headed for Cartagena, a two-hour drive down the coast. Scott Emlong and Little Joe rode in one car with a pair of Colombians, while Ralph Armendariz and the remaining three Colombians occupied the other. The taxis would maintain their distance, keeping the money spread out for security reasons.

As the three couriers and Colombians motored to Cartagena with the money, Leonel Gomez was showing Jimmy Chagra and Peter Kruschewski a portion of the load. The pot was as advertised. In fact, Jimmy wanted to take home a sample for Jack Stricklin and Mike Halliday, but Peter advised against it. Why take the risk? Jimmy, of course, would not be deterred.

The boat was a fishing trawler of about ninety feet, cleverly disguised in rust and grime. No one with the slightest concern about personal safety or hygiene would dare to board her. It was a tub of shit, with all the amenities of a dumpster and a *sail-by* date that had long since expired. But as the captain explained, she would be hiding in plain sight among an endless armada of ugly fishing boats. Interestingly, Ralph Armendariz never had the opportunity to inspect the vessel that would carry him and the load to Boston. Had he been privy to her unfortunate condition, he may well have elected to swim home. By the time he laid eyes on her four weeks later, however, it would be far too late to argue the point.

That same night, for the first and only time, all the players converged in a Cartagena Hotel room. Leonel Gomez had rented the entire floor and armed guards were posted throughout. Accompanying Leonel was a weather-beaten Englishman and a rotund Colombian with an armload of navigational charts. The Colombian was introduced as the ship's captain and navigator. The Englishman oversaw the interests of the boat they had leased for a reported $100,000. He too was an experienced seaman—a shrimper who mostly kept to local waters.

Jimmy, Peter, and the captains spent the next several hours discussing all things maritime. They plotted the route of travel, ruminated about weather and the estimated duration of the voyage. They agreed on a rendezvous point just outside territorial waters and well out of sight of the Massachusetts coastline.

When everyone was satisfied, the money was finally exchanged, glasses were raised, and the wheels began turning on both sides of the Atlantic.

MOTHER LODE

RALPH ARMENDARIZ

The next day, after the money was exchanged, we all went our separate ways. Jimmy Chagra, Peter Kruschewski, Scott Emlong, and Little Joe were all headed to Boston. The Colombians drove me back to Barranquilla. Jimmy Chagra actually sent his own brother-in-law down to Colombia to act as the hostage. But I only saw him once. I was all alone down there—just me and the Colombians.

We passed the Puerto Galleon and went to a place called The Rodeo, which is like a little resort that people go to vacation right on the beach. On the road heading in, there weren't any kind of buildings or shops or anything. It's like the middle of nowhere, and all of a sudden, you come into this community, and there was a hotel, right across the street from the beach.

I had the whole fifth floor. Nobody else stayed on that floor but me. I had a huge room with four beds—one was even a bunk bed. There was a pretty good-size bathroom. My window looked over a side street. It wasn't like the Puerto Galleon, but it was clean.

I was starting to get more comfortable with the Colombians. They called me Don Rafa. Antonio did most of the driving, and there was a young guy named Toto that I got along with pretty well. The other two didn't talk much. Their job was to make sure nothing happened to me. They watched me every minute. Anything I wanted—hookers, pot, booze—they provided it. We hardly went anywhere except to see the pot. But one night they did take me out to dinner.

It was a beat-up little restaurant—rotten floor, metal tables like in Mexico. I went to the bathroom by myself, and they had a trough, so I'm just pissing there, and this old man comes next to me, and he asks me, "You're an American?"

"No," I said, "Colombiano."

"No, you're American. I can tell. Do you like hashish?" Then he pulled out a brick from his back pocket and says, "I've got 4,000 pounds of this. I got a landing strip. I'll front it to you."

"No, I don't do that kind of stuff. I'm a Colombian, and I'm here on vacation."

"I don't believe that. I come into this restaurant quite often, so if you change your mind, I might see you around."

So he just gave me chunk of it. Damn good hash. I told the Colombians about it, and they just said, "You're not going back there again." And we never did. But that's how easy it is to make a big score down there.

When they would come and take me to see the pot, there were at least four or five armed Colombians in the car. We'd be driving down the highway, and we'd see an oncoming car, and they'd all pull out their guns and cock them. I'd look around going, "What are you guys doing?"

They said, "Well, that might be one of the families we're feuding with. Looks like one of their cars. We just want to be ready."

I said, "Well, give me a gun."

"No, you don't need one. We'll take care of you."

So we'd be driving on the highway, and all of a sudden Antonio would just pull over to the shoulder and out of nowhere there was this little cement hut. It had a porch area coming over it that was thrown together with twigs and bark on the rooftop. If you weren't looking for that little hut, you would drive by and never know it was there. But that was the only way to get to the pot. You had to go through a couple of armed guys.

From there, we had to walk. We went out behind the hut and took a little drop down an embankment into a dry ditch. The embankment was high enough so if you're walking through it, nobody really could see you from the highway. Then it goes through a little tunnel underneath the highway, and we end up in a big open field on one side and a banana plantation on the other. There was a dirt road in between.

The banana trees just went on forever. We walked down that road about a hundred yards and started hearing whistles, like a bird. They were more or less announcing to everybody that somebody's on the road. Then, all of a sudden, we took a hard turn into the banana trees and maybe fifteen, twenty yards in, we came to a clearing. That's where the pot was. I don't know how they got in there because you couldn't drive a truck. They must have done it with some kind of box container, wheelbarrows or something.

That first morning, I remember it was really clear and sunny. We came walking in, and I'm looking at all these guys, and they were all natives. They weren't dressed like you or me or the other Colombians. They were barefoot, just some kind of towel or garment across their crotch. It was hot and humid, so they had no shirts on. They just lived there in the banana field. They had a little encampment with their tents and their fire pits made up with rocks to do their cooking.

When we first go walking in, I see the pallets piled up with fresh bricks—not even wrapped yet. And there's this ray of sunlight coming down through the trees right on one of the pallets—it was a spotlight, shining right on those bricks like they were electric. You could see the red and gold that ran all through it. Beautiful. You could get high just smelling it. It's a sight I will never forget. And I remember thinking if I could get this pot to Boston, we were going to make a lot of money.

I went down there every day while they were bringing in the pot. They'd brick it up, wrap it in plastic, and stuff it into coffee sacks. Toto, he was a young kid about nineteen. He went everywhere with me. He was the only one I really trusted. Anyway, he would get a big old chunk of pot, and he would just light it. And he would walk around with me, and we'd just breathe it in. He always had that thing lit.

We put up a pretty sturdy post and rigged a scale. I would weigh each one of the burlap sacks and put a mark on it. I didn't want them to keep re-weighing the same sacks and letting me think that there was more poundage than there really was. It was a working situation. We had a deadline with the mother ship on a certain day, and everybody was working their ass off to make it happen.

One night a couple of weeks later we drove into Santa Marta to receive a phone call from Jimmy. There are five Colombians in the car, plus me. The car's full. We're driving into Santa Marta, and we're going to Leonel's house where his mom and family live in a neighborhood—nothing special, just a lot of small houses.

As we're approaching the house about four blocks away, I see people standing on every corner and Leonel was telling me, "Give them some bucks when they come up to the window." Jack made sure I had money, so I'd throw them fifty, a hundred. We must have made three or four different stops paying off people before we got to his house. They had it surrounded, they were watching, and they were armed.

We go in and sit down and the whole family is there. I know Spanish, so we're talking about off-the-wall shit. Then we get the phone call. I tell Jimmy, "We're still weighing. I haven't been given the exact date the ship would be out there for loading or when we were gonna be ready. I'm at 29,000 or 30,000 pounds, and there's still more out there. But it won't be long now."

He said, "Does everything seem cool—you're not too visible, are you?"

"I'm definitely not visible. They don't know who I am. The Colombians keep me pretty well hid—five guys in a car. You're not gonna be singled out too much."

"Well, I might not talk to you again before you leave."

I said, "These guys will let you know when we're gone. It looks like we're getting close."

I think another week or so went by, maybe less. I finally finished weighing out all the pot. When we got down to the end, we just started throwing loose pot into coffee bags. We were out of time. The boat was waiting.

The Colombianos had a stake-side truck—I have no idea how they got it in there, but I'd say it was probably two-and-a-half ton. The bed maybe sixteen feet, pretty good size, pretty wide too. We started loading the pot on to take to the beach on this narrow dirt road—more like a path. We loaded the first truck about noon on a Saturday.

About two pm, it started raining hard. So, now this dirt road is all muddy. They thought, "We'll just put less bales on the truck, and maybe we can get it to the beach." Well, the truck got stuck. Now we've got a dilemma because the ship's out there. You could see it, a little speck on the ocean.

I told them, "We're gonna have to figure out something. This is going to get loaded one way or the other—even if we have to hand carry it to the beach." It was probably less than a hundred yards away. But it would have been a lot of work.

About an hour and a half went by, and here they come with a tractor. I don't know where they got it. But we were able to load up the truck with more bales now, and the tractor would pull it to the beach, and we'd unload it. Then the tractor would pull up behind the truck and pull it backwards—there was nowhere to turn around on the little path.

We worked all night. The next morning, the boats hadn't started coming in to take the pot out to the mother ship. It's about eight in the morning, and I'm sitting there on this huge pile of pot. I have a carbine. By now I have a 9-mm Toto got for me. I threatened to shoot him if he told anybody about it. But I wasn't going on that boat without a gun.

So I'm sitting on the beach guarding the pot. It was a pretty remote place, but anybody that came walking down that beach—they never got past me. Once they saw the pot, we couldn't let them go. So I would put them to work. There were a few that came by, and I stopped all of them. I paid them, of course, so nobody got too upset.

The Colombians had these three wooden boats. I would say they were maybe eighteen feet long and the sidewalls came up really high. They kind of tapered on both ends like a big canoe, and the motor was in the middle. They were very deep. I don't know where they got them—maybe they used them to move bananas, but they held a lot of pot.

So they bring the boats right up close to the beach, and the Colombians would carry the bales on their shoulders and walk out into the ocean and throw it up to two or three guys on the boat. What happened is, the ocean got so rough there that a couple of guys got washed under. We tried to work through it. We actually loaded a couple of boats, then we decided it wasn't gonna work. So we had to move to another area that was calm, maybe 300 or 400 yards further down the beach. So we moved it again with the trucks and the tractor—very time-consuming.

We'd been up all night already. It was still raining a little bit, but things had calmed down. Sun's coming out, and we're finally moving the pot to the mother ship. I didn't get on the boat until the last load late Sunday afternoon, and that's when I look back and see all of the guys on the beach. Most of them are lying down—totally exhausted. They had given me a special package for the trip home—hand picked buds, really good shit.

The last boatload didn't have that much pot. Maybe fifteen, twenty bales. I rode out on it with Toto and Antonio (the cab driver). We get up to the mother ship, and it's an all-metal, ninety-footer. Has a flat back with a winch. It's a shrimper, that's what it is. We pull up to the side of the boat and start throwing the pot over, but we're having problems because the swells are throwing us around. We finally get all the bales on, and they throw my bags up there. Toto got on first. He had to time it just right before the boats separated again. He made it pretty easy. Then Antonio tried to jump, and the Colombians had to reach out and catch him.

There was no more pot on the boat. We didn't have anything to really stand on so you had to step up to the ledge to get a good jump. We were being thrown around pretty good. One of the guys had to hold onto me. And you had to time it just right. Right after we separated, just as we were coming back together—that was the moment.

As we were separating, I put my foot up there and got ready to jump, but when we came together, we banged so hard that I slipped and ended up hanging feet first right between the two boats. I was barely holding on when the Colombians yanked me onto the deck. They might have saved my life. If I'd been caught between those two boats when they came back together, I would have been flattened.

The name on the back of the mother ship is "Olympic Flame." It was old and rusty and smelled like a sewer. The hull was filled with pot and there were bales in the back cleaning area, even the icebox area. I had a bed down by the engine room, some of the guys just slept on the pot.

The boat came with two captains—a Colombian captain who worked for Leonel, and a British captain who came with the boat. I think he lived on the boat. But the Colombian captain was in charge—it was his crew. And he was the navigator.

Toto and Antonio were Leonel's guys—they came with me on the boat. Toto—he was a good kid, pretty smart and very tough. Antonio I didn't trust. Then there was a guy named Glen who took care of the engines and another guy named Tomas who helped with the engines and did the cooking. There were a couple more. I don't remember their names.

Except for the captains, there was not one guy who looked like he belonged on a boat. They didn't have the right clothes, the right shoes—nothing. The whole crew looked like they'd just come from the disco in their party clothes. If anybody ever got close enough to see these guys they would know right away that none of them were fishermen. It was an odd sight to see this dirty, rusty fishing boat run by guys in loud clothes and dancing shoes.

TRAVELIN' MUSIC

Here's what we knew. Ralph Armendariz was on a boat somewhere in the Atlantic Ocean headed for the North Shore of Boston, Massachusetts, carrying what Jimmy's best guess pegged at around 35,000 pounds of Colombian marijuana. The boat had departed Colombia on the twentieth of June, and was targeted to arrive in the Boston area around the middle of July.

Here's what we didn't know. The North Shore of Boston, Massachusetts, might as well have been a foreign country. We were a collection of desert rats raised in a sea of sand on a river of mud. And we spent every summer in exactly the same place we spent every winter. We were a long way from our comfort zone.

I travelled to Boston with Jack Stricklin, Billy Russell, and Johnny Milliorn. Some of the crew was already there and a few would arrive later. We drove to the Midland/Odessa airport to avoid prying eyes at El Paso International. Jack and Billy were jumping bail. Their case was still in the pre-trial phase with the lawyers doing everything in their power to delay the court date. But travelling without permission would not be looked upon kindly. A three-hour drive through a patch of desert ugly enough to embarrass a landfill seemed a wise precaution.

I didn't think it was my place to ask a lot of questions, but I knew exactly what was on the line. Jack Stricklin and Billy Russell were looking at eighteen months to two years of prison time. Jack owed investors close to $400,000. If the deal didn't go down, he'd be hard-pressed to make enough to live on, much less repay the debt. If we got busted, there would be no one to make our bail. We were flying without a net.

Johnny pushed the needle past a hundred, determined to top his personal best. Jack was up front riding shotgun, taking his usual road-trip nap. I held on tight in the back seat, where Billy looked over the books. There remained a trust issue between Jack, Jimmy, and Peter, and all parties agreed they would be comfortable with Billy Russell doing the accounting.

We flew to Boston without incident and checked into a hotel close to Logan International. Jimmy Chagra and Peter Kruschewski were there to meet us. Jimmy had in his possession a sample of the pot he had brought back from Colombia. It was probably less than an ounce, but it would have been worth five years to the Department of Justice.

"Well, fire it up Jimmy. Let's see what all the fuss is about."

Within minutes, the Colombian pot announced itself to be as advertised: a clean, full-bodied high that lent a chillingly clear perspective to the object of our endeavor. We had travelled nearly 2,000 miles to meet a fishing boat full of pot that was crossing a vast ocean at the height of hurricane season in search of a tiny blip on a chart few of us could decipher. The big boat would then be met by smaller boats that would haul several thousand pounds at a time straight into the high-season on one of the most densely populated coastlines in America where it would be unloaded God-knows-where in the dead of night, transferred onto small trucks and carried to larger trucks that would then deliver it to locations from Atlanta to Pittsburgh to be staged for distribution.

This wasn't a fifteen-minute offload on a lonesome desert road. We were laying siege to the North Shore of Massachusetts. What could possibly go wrong? I decided to take another hit.

Ralph Armendariz:

On the second day out in the evening, somebody went to get some water out of the faucet for cooking. Nothing. We had no water. Glen came to me, and he said, "You know what? I think we're out of water."

I said, "How the fuck can we be out of water?"

He said, "When they filled the tank, I think it leaked into the hull. When I went down to the engine room, I could hear water sloshing underneath."

Where the galley was, there was a stairway going down. As you got to the bottom, there were four bunks and a doorway that went to the engine room. The flooring where the bunks were was made of wood planks.

I went down there with Glen and sure enough, you could hear water sloshing against the planks, and you could see it spilling out onto the floor. Maybe we could pump it out, but we couldn't drink it—it was mixed with diesel and rust and seawater. There were probably rats in there too.

There was a hatch over by the bunks—about a twelve-inch diameter flange with nuts and bolts that looked pretty rusted. I asked Glenn, "What's that?"

"That hatch probably opens into the water tank."

"Let's take it off. See what's left in there."

We had some open socket wrenches, but we couldn't loosen the damn bolts, so we used some oil that they had for the diesel. We worked all night to get them off. It was a pain in the ass. We were all in our underwear by that time, we were sweating so much. The Colombians wore bikini underwear—all paisley-colored and bright colors. I wore boxers. I wasn't used to the idea of guys wearing panties.

After we got the thing off, we got a bucket with some rope and dropped it in that hole and tried to scrape it along. We could hear it hit bottom. We would drag it along and pull it up and get a little bit of water. We worked at that for hours. We did get some water out. We maybe filled up a small container. But it wasn't enough. We had a dilemma.

The next morning, after we'd been working on this shit all night, we go up to the top deck—the area where the wheel was, the windows, chart table, navigation area. You had four or five swivel stools in front of the windows right by the navigation area and the wheel. So, we all meet up there, and the Colombian captain says, "I don't know what we're gonna do without water. We can't drink, we can't cook, can't shower. We try to make it, and we could all die out here."

I looked at Toto, and all I did was nod my head. He had hidden the 9-mm on board. I just nodded at him, and he left and went and got it. When he came back with it, they all just looked at him and got really pissed off that I had a gun on board. I didn't care.

I told the Colombian captain, "You're sixty-years old. You've been on the ocean your whole life, and I'm sure you've run into difficult circumstances that you had to deal with. You're the captain, and they entrusted you with all this merchandise and money. There's a lot at risk here—a lot to lose—a big investment has been made, people are waiting. And I can guarantee you this boat's going to Boston."

He said, "I'm the captain, and I say we're not going."

I asked him, "What's your plan?"

"My plan is to go back to Santa Marta."

"And the pot?"

"We'll throw it in the ocean."

I said, "No, that plan's not gonna fly." And then I cocked the 9-mm. "If you don't want to do it, he can drive this boat." I pointed to the British captain. "If we all perish, then we perish. But this boat is going to Boston."

SURF & TURF

After returning from Colombia, Peter Kruschewski went home to Michigan and immediately dispatched several of his crew to Boston. Scott Emlong was back home just long enough to pick up his car and head immediately to the North Shore to begin searching for suitable real estate. Another member of Peter's crew, Dave Thomas, had also been sent ahead to deliver Peter's Dodge Power Wagon and Formula boat. They set up shop at the King's Grant Motor Inn on Route 1 and began to explore the beachfront rental market.

Dave Thomas was a boat guy, having spent a good deal of his free time on Lake Michigan. He had gone to work for Peter and proven himself on several significant deals. I got to know Dave Thomas and Scott Emlong fairly well during my time at the shore.

Scott was unabashedly self-absorbed. He knew exactly how pretty he was and understood how to exploit it. He had done a little modeling, thought about trying the movies, maybe writing a book. He shared his dreams as openly as he shared his pot. And he wasn't the least bit self-conscious about the love he shared with himself. He carried a man purse and spent his free time at the Roman Health Spa. Everybody liked him—he was fun to be around. And he did his job.

Dave Thomas was the serious one—in my opinion, the best guy in Peter's crew by far. He was confident, smart, and totally focused. He had been involved in the previous summer's hash deal and knew the area as well as anyone, including Peter. He was familiar with exactly the kind of house we would need, and he understood exactly how hard it would be to find.

Peter Kruschewski's idea was to rent three houses suitable for the offload. That meant three oceanfront houses with enough privacy to conduct business unseen. The season was already in full swing, and the pickings were slim. They explored listings on Cape Ann, but the houses were too close together. They checked out a place in Manchester that was advertised as beachfront, but turned out to be across the street from the water. They scoured Rockport and. Gloucester—everything they saw was either too far from the water's edge or wedged so tightly between neighbors as to render night work impossible.

Jimmy Chagra was not happy with the results. He called Peter Kruschewski and told him to catch the next plane to Boston to find out why his guys weren't getting the job done. After several days scouring the shore, Peter began to understand the problem. But the clock was ticking, and we couldn't very well ask the boat to wait at anchor while we shopped for a suitable offload site.

Ralph Armendariz

> We knew it rained a lot on the ocean—you could see it, just like out in the desert. Every time we saw rain, we headed toward rain. We had buckets and tubs. We plugged the drain holes in the little deck behind the navigation area. We had a hose so we could siphon it right into a tank we had.
>
> We'd collect a pretty good amount, but when you look at it, there's all this crap floating around. We'd get the water out of there with plastic pitchers and boil it and put it in the icebox which was kept locked at all times. When anybody drank water, everybody drank water. And we got one cup of coffee a day. The Colombians had to have their coffee.

The boat was only moving five or six knots an hour. That's not very fast. It was an old boat. We could have broken down at any time. I'd go down and listen to the engines run. *Clink, clink, clank, clank.* We had to stop a couple of times while Glen worked on them. The stove caught fire twice. It was a death trap.

One day I'm just laying out on the back deck smoking a joint, and Glen comes up to me and says, "I've gotta talk to you."

I said, "Okay."

He said, "Let's go in the galley."

I got up and went with him, and he says, "Listen, I haven't told you because I didn't know what you would do. The other night I had to take a piss. I woke up about two-thirty or three in the morning, and I walked out, and I smelled smoke. It wasn't that anyone was smoking cigarettes. It smelled like motor smoke."

I said, "And?"

He says, "I walked down to the engine room, and the cables from the batteries leading to the diesel engines were on fire."

I said, "Where was Tomas?"

He said, "He was asleep. Smoked too much pot."

Tomas was supposed to stay awake all night and watch the engine. He and Glenn took shifts. He had the night shift.

Glenn said, "If I hadn't woken up to take that piss, we could have blown up. I got a fire extinguisher, and I put it out, but I didn't wanna tell you right away because I thought you might shoot the son of a bitch."

I said, "Well, I'm not gonna shoot him. But you're gonna get everybody together right now, and you're gonna take care of this—he's your guy. If you don't take care of it, then I will. I'm not gonna put up with any of this. There's too much at stake."

They come on down, even the British captain, and

we're all in the galley. They put this guy right at the end of the table, and they told him, "If we catch you smoking pot at any time, we're gonna throw you in the ocean."

And Tomas started crying, "I've got kids. I've got a wife. I've got a family."

They said, "Well, if you love them, don't smoke pot. That's all. If you do, we will throw you in the ocean."

I didn't say one word.

About a week after Peter Kruschewski arrived from Michigan, Scott Emlong showed him a house he had found at Folly Point, overlooking a small, deep-water cove. It was relatively secluded, but sat about seventy, very rocky feet above the water. It wouldn't be easy to move the pot up that hill. The other issue was that the house was completely made of glass. Peter decided it might make a good secondary offload sight and instructed Scott to rent it immediately and then to find another house— not necessarily on the water, but one that might house the crew coming in from Texas.

Scott quickly located and secured a suitable place in Manchester, no lease required. Meanwhile, Peter was closing in on an oceanfront home at Stevens Point, which he ultimately managed to lease from a local doctor. He dubbed it "suitable backup #1."

The negotiations on the property at Folly Cove were proving problematic. The rental agent required more references than Peter was willing to provide, so Scott Emlong and Dave Thomas were instructed to rent the house in their own name, using personal references to secure the lease. They weren't overjoyed at the prospects, but there weren't a lot of options. They executed the agreement and we had "suitable backup #2."

Peter moved himself, his boat, and his wife into the house at Stevens Point. Dave Thomas imported his girlfriend to lend a bit of legitimacy to Folly Cove. His job now was to begin shopping for boats while Scott and Peter continued to search for viable oceanfront property.

I stayed with Jack Stricklin and Billy Russell the first night. I thought I might remain in their heady company for the duration. But the next day, Jack and Billy moved into a comfortable little cottage on a tree-lined street in Lynn. And Johnny Milliorn and I moved to the house that Scott Emlong had rented in Manchester. Mike Halliday, Johnny Milliorn, and seven or eight members of the crew were already in residence.

We referred to the house as "The Barracks" because it was spartan to the point of empty. No beds, no towels, no chairs— just floors, walls and a roof. But it was bordered on three sides by a ten-foot hedge, and sat back a good sixty feet from the road. It would be an ideal staging house for the big U-Haul trucks that were scheduled to carry up to 10,000 pounds apiece.

The house itself was nothing special—a one-story siding and shingle ranch with linoleum floors, ugly wallpaper, and bugs. Grow up in the desert and you learn to coexist with a diverse collection of crawlers. But these were a juicier variety of bug— and a little on the aggressive side. War was quickly declared.

There were two small bedrooms and a bath and a half. Most of us ended up sleeping in the large living room just off the kitchen. We made ourselves as comfortable as we could with air mattresses and sleeping bags, bought a boom box, and stocked the fridge with beer.

Among the crew was a guy named Steve Andrade who had worked at one time for the phone company. Our story was that we were a southern crew sent north to upgrade the area's phone lines. In Texas, a cover like that would never have worked. Guys would be climbing the pole to show you exactly where they thought the trouble was. And then they'd spend the rest of the day drinking beer and watching you pretend to work.

In Massachusetts, the cover was hardly even necessary.

Nobody gave a shit. People seemed to take deliberate steps to stay out of our way. I guess when you live your life in such close proximity to your neighbor, ignoring them can become somewhat habitual. Especially in an area that sees a summer migration the size of the North Shore.

The next morning, Johnny Milliorn drove me to Peabody ("Pibidy" to the locals). I was to purchase a used truck he had located. Two similar vehicles had already been bought. Jack was running out of guys without prior convictions, so I was elected to buy the third of three vans. It was a step van—a smaller version of a UPS truck.

Massachusetts was one of the first states to adopt no-fault insurance, which meant it was next to impossible to purchase a vehicle under an assumed name. Proper ID was required. No getting around it without a really good fake ID, which we had neither the time nor money to obtain. So I sucked it up, signed the papers, and drove off in my used step van. If it were ever seized, my name would be all over the paperwork. So much for plausible deniability.

MOVING PARTS

It was the next morning when we got our first look at the glass house on Folly Cove. I was with Mike Halliday and Buzzy Harrison. We were meeting Jack Stricklin, Billy Russell, Jimmy Chagra, and Peter Kruschewski to take a look. As Dave Thomas and Scott Emlong (who had taken up residence) showed us around, I couldn't help but chuckle at the irony of running a shipload of pot through a transparent house in a place called Folly Cove. No one would ever believe it.

The house was set on a little bluff, seventy feet or so above the water. It resided on several acres, most of which were trees and native shrubs. It stood about a hundred yards back from the highway, well-hidden by the trees. On one side was a neighboring estate, which sat on several acres further toward the point. About eighty yards distant on the other side, just around a bend in the highway, was a cutout where cars could turn in and overlook the cove. It was a popular spot for local scuba divers.

The rocky cliff presented a formidable obstacle. Jimmy and Peter were convinced we could form a human chain and hand the bales from man to man right to the top. Jack and Billy wondered out loud just how many fatalities we were willing to accept. Handling heavy bales on slick rocks in the dead of night on the side of a wet cliff was a very Jimmy Chagra solution. Sanity would fortunately prevail.

Mike Halliday had separated himself from the pack and was

smoking a joint as he surveyed the property. He climbed down the rocks and back up again, then went back down for another look. He noticed a small gorge that split the rock all the way to the top. He climbed up and looked at the trees closest to the narrow ravine. When he finally rejoined the rest of us, he wore a shit-eating grin from ear to ear. "This place is perfect—it's fucking Xanadu!"

Everyone had their opinion about the place, but Mike Halliday was the first to really see it through the eyes of a smuggler. That's why he was there. He knew at a glance we would find no better spot to conduct our business.

Mike's plan was to anchor a two-man platform to the rocks on the far side of the gorge and attach a small dock to hold the pot. Then we'd tie a rope to the apple tree at the top. Using a simple basket or cargo nets, we would haul the bales right up the cliff—easy-peasy.

Everyone agreed it made more sense than a chain of fools. And everyone had an opinion on how best to build it. Peter was quick to remind us that Folly Cove was just a secondary house—he was still shopping for a better alternative. We were beginning to discover a careful streak in Peter that seemed to be widening by the day. To him, the perfect landing spot meant finding a house on a remote island, connected to the mainland by a series of caves, and inhabited by a tribe of natives who lived to carry heavy bales on their heads. We weren't going to wait around while he chased that rainbow. Jimmy and Jack overruled his objections, and Folly Cove was designated for the primary offload.

Over the next couple of days we made several visits to the glass house as we began to refine the plan. On the morning construction was to begin, Mike decided it would be a good idea to look over the property one more time. We grabbed coffee and headed over for a last look.

When we got there, Mike lit up his morning doobie and

headed off to survey the grounds while we went over the list of materials with Dave Thomas and Scott Emlong. Within a few seconds we heard screaming. We quickly ran to the edge of the cliff thinking Mike had fallen. And there he stood at the bottom of the ravine with his hands spread like Moses at the Red Sea, yelling, "What the fuck happened to my water!"

Ralph Armendariz

Somehow, day-by-day, we kept moving. I don't know how many days went by, but it happened pretty quickly—we hit a storm, might have been a typhoon. We were all sitting in the navigation area, and the water was just slamming the windows. Huge swells—the boat would rise up out of the water, then drop twenty or thirty feet. We were constantly at the wheel, trying to hold our course. We didn't have sophisticated navigation equipment. The Colombian captain used a sextant—that's all he used. But we really didn't give a shit where we were headed. We were just trying to stay afloat.

I didn't think we were gonna make it through that night. The ocean was throwing our little boat around like a toy. We'd get to the bottom of a swell, and water would cover the front of the boat. Then we'd look up, and here came a wall right down on top of us. Over and over it would happen. And the only thing you can do is hold on and pray.

We're getting beat up. We can't even stand. Wherever we walk, we're banging against walls. We took turns at the wheel. I kept thinking the damn thing was gonna break because there was so much torque on it. I could hardly even turn the son of a bitch. And even when I was holding onto the wheel, I'd be thrown around. I just kept thinking to myself, "Oh, my God, how many times is this boat gonna be able to take this? How many times am I gonna be able to take it?"

By this point I had a lot of uncertainty if we were gonna make it or not. That storm was probably the scariest thing that ever happened to me. But even if we survived it, there was always concern with the stove, with the battery cables, with the water, with the crew.

Each time one of these things happened, you'd wonder, what's it gonna be tomorrow? What's gonna happen tonight? Is this piece of shit boat gonna keep running? And me and the Colombian captain, we did not get along, because I'd threatened him. I had to. There was no other way around it. I was not going back to Santa Marta. I was not throwing the pot in the ocean. But the way things were going there was a real chance it would all end up in the ocean anyway—and us right along with it.

The tide comes in. The tide goes out. This is life on the shore. That a group of earthbound apple-knockers from El Paso, Texas had failed to account for the twelve-foot tide was a testament to our landlocked mentality.

"Are you sure this happens every day?"

Undaunted by the setback, we adapted and overcame. The first thing we did was attach a small stationary platform to the face of the cliff—big enough for two people to stand on, high enough to be unaffected by the highest tide, and sturdy enough to anchor a small floating dock connected by a hinged gangway that would rise and fall with the tide. The dock itself was made of half-inch plywood over six-foot Styrofoam blocks. It was covered with a waterproof, non-slip surface. By simply removing the hinge pins, the dock and gangway could be easily set up and removed. The end result was something that looked more like a bath toy than an actual floating dock. But it held our weight and it would hold much more.

Like opening night on Broadway, the critics were in the house.

The strongest opinions were reserved for the rope and basket intended to haul the goods. Simply stated, it wouldn't work. It sagged like an old plow horse, and there was no saving it. Buzzy Harrison, an ex-navy seaman, suggested using a cable and pulley. The critics agreed. So Mike and Buzzy set to work attaching one end of a three-eighths-inch cable to the apple tree on the topside, the other to heavy-duty eyebolts firmly embedded in the rocks below. A simple come-along pulled the cable tight, and *voila!* The Great Walenda himself could have walked that wire.

But the naysayers would not be silenced. Though they had generally approved of the cable, there was a strong contingent that wanted to employ a block and tackle to make the pulling easier. "No," Mike argued, "it's going to make too much noise, and it's just one more thing that can go wrong. If there's one thing we got plenty of, it's muscle. So shut up and pull the rope!"

The device Mike and Buzzy had fabricated at a local machine shop was basically a hook on two pulleys, covered by a housing to keep the cable from kinking. An eyebolt welded to the top would attach to the rope, which the crew would pull. It was elegant in its simplicity. And more importantly, it was quiet. Mike eventually wrapped the housing in carpet to further deaden the sound. A backup cable was purchased and ready to be put into play should the need arise.

We spent several nights setting up in the dark and running bags of sand up the hill. The guys at the top complained about the effort, which was easily solved by putting more guys at the top. I was assigned to work on the dock with Mike Halliday and Buzzy Harrison. Jack wanted me down there because I was a swimmer—it had been my exercise of choice for several years. I was also a certified scuba diver, though the desert offered little in the way of opportunity. Most of my experience was in the deep end of a swimming pool, but it was experience enough for the job at hand. Setting up the dock and pulley was a pretty simple matter, but you had to get in the water to do it. Mike Halliday, Buzzy Harrison, and I were considered the least likely to drown.

The boat was still a few days from its scheduled arrival. Anxiety stayed well beneath the surface. I was soaking up the scene, enjoying the ocean, and getting acquainted with some of the guys on Peter's crew. I didn't know it at the time, but I later learned there were close to fifty guys up and down the North Shore awaiting the arrival of the mother ship. Some were customers who were kept isolated from the offload locations for obvious reasons. Peter had his own offload crew stationed at Stevens Point. There were boat crews, van drivers, and truck drivers, loaders and un-loaders, gophers and yes-men. I never even came close to meeting everyone. My life revolved around the glass house, The Barracks—and a little dock that rode up and down on the tide like a cork.

As we refined and tinkered with the dock and pulley, the offload boats would come in and out, rehearsing their routes to and from the rendezvous point, which for purposes of CB radio transmission was dubbed "The Rotary."

Dave Thomas and Scott Emlong crewed a relatively new thirty-foot cabin cruiser with a capacity of about 7,000 pounds—her name was *Just A Habit.* Either the hand of fate was dropping breadcrumbs in our path, or someone with an ironic sense of humor was way ahead of us.

Two additional boats, more randomly christened but similar in size, were also rehearsing their runs to the little dock. *Priscilla III* was piloted by a guy everyone called Football Head—his shaved head resembled a pigskin.

"Maybe you should try to grow some laces."

"Man, somebody yells fumble in a crowded theater and you're toast."

Football Head took it in style and gave back most of what he got. His partner was a solidly built Viking woman who had grown up on a boat and could more than keep up with the guys. Her, we didn't kid.

The third boat, *Red Leg,* was to be piloted by another of Peter

Kruschewski's guys—Dan Cacy. Dan had purchased the boat (with Jack's money) and had every intention of becoming its captain. Unfortunately, a full display of his seamanship resulted in significant damage to a local dock. So Brad Dexter, a member of Jack's crew, was put in charge of *Red Leg*. Dan Cacy would remain aboard in a supporting role.

BRAD DEXTER

I grew up on Long Island. So the North Shore was very familiar to me. I was around boats all my life—at least until I got to El Paso. I met my wife in college, and she had known Jack most of her life. That's how he and I got to know each other. I helped out with a few airplane loads and a little driving now and then, but nothing full time. I had just gotten my teaching certificate and my first job teaching physical education and coaching the football team at a junior high. I didn't know shit about football. I was barely able to find twenty-two kids who wanted to play. We got beat a lot.

When Jack came to me before the Boston deal and mentioned boats, I was hooked. You know Jack. He didn't provide many details. But I was off in the summer anyway, and a teacher's paycheck didn't go very far. So I headed to Boston and got set up with some of the other boat guys at a little motel by the marina at Cape Ann.

They put me on the *Red Leg* with Dan Cacy. Dan reminded everyone of Gomer Pyle—a simple, easy-going guy who liked everybody. I remember the guys invited him to play poker one night and he said, "Naw, I couldn't do that."

"Oh, come on, Dan—why not?"

"Because I cheat. And I like you guys too much to cheat you."

I found out later that Dan robbed post offices.

One morning, I'm sitting in the galley. It must have been about seven or eight, and I'm realizing all of a sudden, things are pretty calm. My coffee cup is sitting on the table nice—I don't even have to hold it. And I'm thinking, pretty strange, you know. And one of the Colombians comes and gets me and says, "Come outside."

I walked outside, and he said, "Look at the water." As far as you could see on all sides, the water was just like a sheet, no swells, just a solid sheet totally still. You could see all the way to the farthest horizon, and this ninety-footer was riding on the water like a motorboat. That's how it was moving. And I said, "That's pretty strange."

He said, "Yeah, we're in the Bermuda Triangle."

I said, "I've always heard about that bullshit, but I've never believed any of it."

He said, "I'm telling you, we are in the Bermuda Triangle."

And it was very eerie, God's honest truth, very eerie. And it went on for hours. The crew was freaked out. They were paranoid. They made me paranoid.

In less than twenty-one days, a pair of oceanfront homes had been secured to receive the product. Five inland houses had been rented to shelter the participants and stage the distribution. Three step vans had been bought and serviced. Large U-Haul trucks were rented for distribution. Three twenty-five to thirty-foot cabin cruisers had been purchased, crewed, and fitted for the offload. Radios, police scanners, and binoculars were acquired. Routes to and from the staging houses were rehearsed and frequencies memorized. A dock was built, a pulley system created. And we were nearly broke.

Oh, we spent every nickel, and had to go get some more—we were out of money.

Billy and I called Atlanta and talked to John Hughes and his partner. And I said, "You got any more money?"

And they said, "We gave you everything we had."

I said, "You know anybody?"

And they said, "Yeah, we might. Come on down."

So Billy Russell and I got on a plane, and we went down there to meet with this guy. Jimmy had been hoarding the sample of pot he brought back from Colombia, but I took it from him so the guy could have a little taste. He smoked just enough to know it was the real thing. I told him, "Listen, just ask John—we've been doing business for a long time, and he'll tell you everything you need to know about me."

And John said, "I've made a lot of money with Jack. I wouldn't turn you on to him if I didn't think he was a man you could trust. We've put most of our own money into this thing and it's close—real close."

The guy had $30,000, but he wanted to keep $2,000. I said, "No. I need every dime."

Here I am telling this guy he can't hang on to two grand of his own money. That's how much we needed it. He ended up giving us $29,000. We promised to pay him in product at 3 to 1. That would be close to $90,000 worth of weed—at our price. He stood to make a lot of money.

That guy really saved our ass. If he had turned us down, I have no idea where I would have gone next. I'd have probably sold a kidney.

HIDE & SEEK

Sometime around the middle of July, things started to get serious. The boats went out every night while the crew sat quietly in the house on Folly Cove tuned to their CB radios. After weeks of almost manic activity, all that remained was to sit and wait. The nights were long and anxious.

I can't remember if I was more afraid that we wouldn't find the boat or more terrified that we would. What else was there to do but imagine the worst possible things that could happen? Time is not your friend when you spend it waiting.

There was, of course, money wagered on the exact date of arrival. Jimmy probably had bets with everybody on the crew. He had his money on July 18th—a Friday night, some twenty-eight days since the boat left Colombia.

But July 18th came and went as the pattern began to establish itself. Jimmy would go out on *Just A Habit* with Dave and Scott. *Priscilla III* and *Red Leg* were on station at The Rotary and Peter circled the area in his Formula boat. Our offload boats would troll the designated waters until a few hours before dawn as we sat in silent contemplation, fixed on the lights of Cape Ann and the steady traffic of the shipping channel.

Brad Dexter

If I remember right, *Red Leg* was about a thirty-two foot Richardson—probably from some time in the fifties. It was bigger than what I was used to, but those twin engines are easier to handle than the little boats—you can turn 'em on a dime. I spent a lot of time on the water with Dan. We'd cruise out to The Rotary—the rendezvous point when we were talking on the CBs. We wanted to blend in with the noise.

We'd made a lot of practice runs in the daytime, but when we started going out nights it was a whole different thing—you know, everybody wanted to be the one who found it—a little friendly competition between the boats. Mostly we'd stay out 'til just before dawn, but a couple of nights, it was so foggy out there you couldn't see across your own bow. All you could do was try to find your way home.

We ran into *Just A Habit* one night in the heavy fog—not literally of course. We pulled up close and tried to figure out where we were. You could hear the foghorn at the lighthouse so we kind of navigated by that. When we heard surf crashing into the beach, we knew we were way off course, but the good news was we recognized where we were and got home, no problem. It would have been real embarrassing to run aground.

We'd been out there for six or seven straight nights. But nobody wanted to give up. Jack was positive it was out there. We had a little pool going for the boat that found the trawler. So we kept our eyes open.

Then one night Dan and I are out running grids, and we saw this trawler. We kind of circled around to get it in silhouette and sure enough it was a ninety-foot shrimper—just what we were looking for. We were really excited as we approached that boat.

We were supposed to ask for Ralph. So we pulled up close and started yelling, "Ralph! Ralph!"

These guys must have thought we were crazy. Some boat pulls up in the middle of the ocean and starts yelling at them—I'm surprised they didn't just shoot us.

Right place, right time, wrong boat—I really thought we found it.

RALPH ARMENDARIZ

I think we were still somewhere around the Bermuda Islands. And there's a boat approaching us, a small boat, like maybe a sixteen-footer or something like that, kind of like a motorboat, a couple of people on it, and they were approaching us. So I go inside, and I told the rest of them, "Don't come out here. Let me handle this."

Now the name on the back of our boat was *The Olympic Flame* and there was a beat-up American flag on the post—I put it there. And so this boat's approaching us, and behind me, there's a porthole for the bathroom. All of a sudden, I hear Toto say, "Rafael." He told me in Spanish, "Don't worry, if they approach us, I'll take care of them." And I look back, and he had that 9-millimeter sticking out of the porthole.

I said, "Put the fucking gun away. Let me talk first."

He says, "If they get suspicious, I'm shooting them."

I said, "First of all, they don't know what we have. So calm down, let me try talking first."

They couldn't get too close to us because it was pretty rough. But they got close enough for a conversation. They spoke English. And they said, "Hey, what are you guys up to, man—you out here fishing?"

I said, "Yeah, we just haven't had very much luck."

Actually we had come across a bunch of fishing buoys—they had Japanese markings. We had hauled in a few lines and we got some fish off of it. We didn't see boats anywhere, so we just pulled them in. We probably could have gotten shot for that. They had pretty good-sized fish on there as bait. So we had them sitting on the deck, and we had some hanging off the boom to make it look like, "Hey, we're fishing."

So I told them, "No, we're not having too much luck. We're just gonna travel around the island here a little bit and see how things go for us. Who are you people?"

And they said, "Oh, we're fishermen. We're kind of scouting for a place to call our other boats out to fish."

And I said, "Do we need to move or find another place?"

"No, no," he says. "You're good. We just wanted to see if everything was okay."

They were dressed in fishermen clothes. They didn't look like cops. They said, "Well, have a good day, man. Good luck out here. And if we run across each other's paths, we'll let you know where the fish are."

"Okay, thanks," I said. "We're probably not gonna hang around here too much. We're gonna swing further out."

I told Toto, "See, dumbass, it was just a couple of fisherman. What if you'd have shot them, man?"

The glass house offered a clear view of the ocean, which is a nice way of saying the glass house was a fishbowl with furniture. There were drapes of course, useful at night but suspicious by day. Nobody came to the North Shore in early July to hide behind curtains. The room that offered the best view was the living room, connected to a dining room just off the kitchen. The muted TV and backlit display of the radios were the only source of illumination. But there was enough raw energy in that room to light up a three-ring circus.

Normally there were up to a dozen of us in the house,

though some opted to sit quietly outside. Jack Stricklin and Billy Russell occupied hard chairs up close to the radios. Mike Halliday preferred the easy chair in the corner, and Johnny Milliorn always had a reserved seat. The rest of us made do with whatever surface was available. The smoke-filled room pulsed with the flickering light of a muted TV, while the constant chatter of the police scanners broadcast a sobering reminder of the stakes. But it was our own CBs we were anxious to hear, and they remained stubbornly silent.

Communication between the glass house and the search boats was kept to a minimum. But every transmission sent a bolt of electricity through the room. And just as quickly, the air was totally removed. It's hard to believe you could be so wrung out by sitting and waiting. But this was full-contact waiting—a winner-take-all death match that had so far been fought to a draw.

BITCH FEST

RALPH ARMENDARIZ

Now this might not even be significant to the story, but I'll tell you. Everybody on board was a smoker so we all had cigarettes. But then we ran out—cold turkey. One day, we caught Antonio, the cab driver, out in the back smoking a cigarette.

So we went over there and asked him, "Where'd you get that cigarette?"

"Well," he says, "I got some."

I said, "Where? Where are they?"

And that son of a bitch had a full carton he was keeping hid. So we took them away from him. I told him, "We'll give you a cigarette when we wanna give you a cigarette. You wanna be that guy? You wanna hide them from us and not share them? Okay, fine. Then here, I'll give you one now, and whenever I decide I wanna give you a cigarette, you'll have a cigarette because all of us are gonna have a cigarette!"

That might be an insignificant thing, no big deal, but it was trauma, and it was drama to try and keep the peace on the boat without kicking each other's ass. There was a total of ten of us—the two captains, me, and seven crew. But I ran the show. They knew I wasn't gonna tolerate anything that would keep this deal from happening.

After that, things got a little calmer. No more fires.

We're moving along. We're motoring. So, now, really, it's kind of like the doldrums. Everything's kind of boring. The days were monotonous. We were all really tired. We haven't showered. The only way to clean yourself is with ocean water. We were getting to our limits—starting to act pretty cranky with each other. "Fuck you's" were flying all over the boat.

Back on land, the nerve-rattling nights were offset by loosely woven days. Jack and Jimmy had imported one of their pot pilots for an aerial search. But traffic along the trade routes was so heavy, they might as well have been looking for a splinter in the woodpile.

After seven long nights of futility, the negativity was beginning to surface. A boat overdue by a couple of days might not have been all that uncommon, but as we approached day four, five, and six, ominous feelings were beginning to surface.

Jimmy Chagra openly worried the Colombians would think he had hijacked their load. Jack had to constantly assure customers that everything was moving according to plan, while Billy was knee-deep in the logistics of a deal that had more moving parts than Big Ben. Meanwhile, life in the barracks was a bug rodeo of numbing routine. We would set up. We would wait all night. We would tear down. Rinse and repeat.

I had imagined an adventurous life surrounded by fearless smugglers whose courage and confidence defined the spirit of the pot culture. What I experienced, however, more closely resembled a bridge club—hardly a single member of which could cease bitching long enough to blow up his air mattress.

What the fuck is a clam? It tastes like the ass-end of a garbage disposal.

Did you see the place those guys are living in? It's got beds and couches.

Rotaries? Motherfuckers ought to be called suicide circles the way these people drive.

You can't get chips and salsa anywhere. And what fucking language are they talking, anyway?

We were a bunch of guys in a confined space with little in the way of amenities. We worked all night, slept on the floor, ate takeout around the clock, and shared two dirty bathrooms. We had the shitty end of the stick, and bitching was the only relief. Strangely, there was little conjecture on the fate of Ralph Armendariz and the missing mother ship. No one really wanted to speak out loud the obvious consequence of being lost at sea. So leaking air mattresses were much discussed, as well as the viscosity of a fried clam, not to mention the identity of that six-legged hubcap crawling across the living room floor.

During our time on the shore, we had gotten friendly with several members of Peter Kruschewski's crew. They were more than happy to participate in the daily bitch-fest. If you worked for Peter, you had only one job and that was to obey. But true loyalty turned out to be in short supply among his crew. The Army had taught Peter the fine art of issuing orders. Unfortunately, he learned very little about dealing with the men who received them.

While we waited every night at the glass house in relative comfort, Peter kept his offload crew sequestered in a dark bedroom with strict orders to remain silent. When he wasn't at the house on Stevens Point, he was riding around in a custom-tailored smuggling suit on his hi-speed Formula boat. Peter darted in and out of the search area like a hummingbird. Somehow, the word *chickenshit* always managed to find its way into the conversation.

The days piled up with monotonous regularity as the marine layer hovered over us like a scrim. When you grow up in eternal sunshine, its absence is acutely felt. But the gauzy layer held fast to the humidity, casting a sultry malaise over a tiring crew.

Of course, we all had been to see the summer blockbuster "Jaws."

Those fuckers can sniff out a hangnail, brother. Better not cut yourself shaving before you get in the water.

"Shit," Mike Halliday said, "you can't kill a fucking shark by stuffing a scuba tank down its throat. Sharks don't know how to scuba dive."

I have met few people in my life who could make me laugh like Mike Halliday. Boston was where he and I finally got to know each other, though we had been acquainted for a few years. Like me, Mike embraced the North Shore and its inhabitants. He lived every day with eager fascination, welcoming new information like an old friend. During our long days together, we talked about everything from the Kissinger doctrine to the hallucinogenic properties of the worm in a bottom of Mescal. And just like I could always get a laugh out of Jack Stricklin, Mike Halliday never failed to get a laugh out of me.

It wasn't as if everything Mike said was funny. It was that Mike had a funny way of saying everything. His hands were in constant motion, and he paced, often with his head down, sometimes seeming to walk in place. Suddenly, he would look up and say something so completely out of left field you could only wonder what movie he was watching. Then he would transport that random thought down a winding road and end up at a destination that somehow managed to make perfect sense.

If Mike were trying to be funny, it never would have worked. The kid was a natural. But at his core, Mike Halliday was a smuggler. He endured the nightly ritual, never losing patience or hope. While the crew chose to deal with their frustration by venting in every direction, Mike just fired up another joint and settled in to wait. If the Mexicans had taught him anything, it was that a smuggler's temperament is forged in patience.

BILLY RUSSELL

It was gloomy at times, very gloomy. The business we were in, the business of smuggling, was a business of waiting. You can only do so much to make a thing happen, then you just have to sit back and let it. Jack didn't get down. He didn't focus on the problem as much as he focused on the solution. Whatever it was, he just dealt with it.

Mostly, he was dealing with money—or lack of it. We were renting houses—beachfront houses in the summer and inland houses for staging, boats to offload the mother ship, vehicles for transport. This was no small deal. We were going through $30,000 a week easily. I don't know how he did it, but Jack always managed to come up with more. He was always on, always laughing, always hustling. You couldn't be around him and not feel positive.

You know, we all went up there on the hope of making more money than we ever made in our lives. We were all committed to it because of Jack Stricklin and Mike Halliday. Not because of Jimmy Chagra and not because of Peter Kruschewski—they weren't like us. Jack and Mike were the ones everybody got behind. It never occurred to Jimmy or Peter that loyalty was worth anything. But at that point, it was the only thing holding the deal together.

But you couldn't help thinking about all the things that can go wrong on an ocean.

On the night of July 21st, we gathered as usual. Within a fifteen-mile radius, drivers were standing by their trucks, staging houses were readied for delivery, and customers were preparing to receive their loads. Three boats ran grids in the ocean while a fourth remained just outside the search area. The weather was calm, the moon was nearly full, and the frustration was mounting. Failure had become our routine—the keen edge of anxiety blunted by the boredom of a long and fruitless wait.

All we could do was sit quietly as we pondered the possibility of failure and what comes next. In the beginning, we were more worried about getting caught than being left empty-handed. But the more we thought about a tiny boat on a vast ocean, the more we tilted toward a nightmare at sea.

Like previous nights, this one would end with empty boats headed back to the marina. As we were preparing to return to The Barracks, I was one of the last of the crew to leave the house. Billy Russell and Jack Stricklin were staying behind to meet with Jimmy Chagra who had gone out on *Just A Habit* with Dave Thomas and Scott Emlong.

On my way to the step van, I happened to glance up the footpath that connected the adjacent property. Striding down the worn path was a small man in khakis and a cable-knit sweater, sporting a friendly smile and a half-empty highball.

I stammered a nervous greeting and said, "Hey, I hope the party wasn't too loud. We tried to keep it down."

But the little man just held out his right hand and said, "Hi, I'm the neighbor, Don Ferris. I just came over for a drink."

It's four in the morning and the Welcome Wagon comes rolling in for cocktails? Say this for Yankee hospitality: it is without curfew. By now, Jack and Billy had come to the rescue. The guys in the van were in no mood to make nice with the neighbor. Since I had just met him, Jack indicated that Mike and I should stay. The rest of the guys went back to The Barracks.

Don Ferris was a man in his early thirties with a round red face and longish hair, which he constantly swept from his forehead. He was a cherub who screamed Yankee all the way down to his boat shoes. Don may have stood 5'2" on a good day, while Jack, Billy and I averaged about 6'3". Mike was a bit closer to the ground. It was obvious that Don was uncomfortable standing in our midst, so we got our drinks and took seats. Don Ferris preferred to stand and would remain so for the duration. We were eye-to-eye, and that was just where he wanted us.

His full name was Donald Fitzgerald Ferris. He claimed to be a member of the Kennedy clan. I had only been on the North Shore for three weeks, and here I was having cocktails with a Kennedy! And this particular Kennedy anointed himself the black sheep of the family.

Donald Ferris had been an officer in the Marine Corps and served in Vietnam. He was unmarried and had just completed his third year at Harvard Law, though he had no idea what he would do with the rest of his life. And yes, thank you, he would have a hit of that joint you just lit. Billy Russell fired it up and passed it to him just to see how he would react. We all tried not to be too obvious about our interest. If he had been offended by the offer, or run away in mortal fear of being arrested, I'm not sure what we would have done. But Don took himself a couple of healthy hits and passed the joint.

Scott Emlong, Dave Thomas, and Jimmy Chagra soon returned from Cape Ann and joined the impromptu party. Scott and Dave had already met Don, who was still on his feet but beginning to list. He talked about his tour in Vietnam and his life on the shore. Name-dropping seemed to be a specialty, though we knew none of the names he tossed in our direction.

Don gossiped and drank his way toward dawn without a hint of suspicion in his attitude. The threat-meter was headed back to green. It looked like he was just an amiable drunk who decided to pop in for cocktails at four am. Sometime around dawn, he realized it was getting late. He had to go to work in the morning, he said. He was interning with the U.S. Attorneys office out of Boston.

Holy shit.

Ralph Armendariz

We finally get close to the area we think are the right coordinates. We had been told to be looking out for four to six lights. And so that's what we were looking for.

I asked the captain, "Are we close to those coordinates?"

He said, "We're real close."

And I said, "Well, we should start seeing something."

Then I see these lights, and there's four or five of them, but they're kind of scattered or separated because it's the ocean. I'm thinking, "Is that them?"

I told the captain, "Take a look out there, man. Is that within our coordinates?"

He says, "I can't really tell, but from where we are in comparison to where those lights are, it doesn't look like it's in our quadrant."

I said, "Well, maybe we should go investigate."

So we did, and it turned out it was just a bunch of other people fishing out there. They were yelling at us. They said, "Hey, we have nets out here, man!" They kind of got pissed. So we got out of there and went back into international waters. We just sat there talking for the rest of the night. *Are they still looking for us? Was that the right coordinates?* The captain told me, "Man, the coordinates that they gave us, that's right where we were at."

I said, "Okay, let's try it again tomorrow night."

PARTY TIME

JACK STRICKLIN

I wasn't worried. I didn't have time to be worried. I was chasing money 24/7. I had customers and crew up and down the North Shore. And there was never a minute when one of them didn't have a problem. So on top of the money, I was dealing with every chickenshit issue that came up. I wasn't going to add to that by worrying about the boat. That was out of my control.

I knew the crew needed to blow off some steam. All you can do is give 'em a little break, and they'll be fine. But the guys wanted a night in the Combat Zone and that was never going to happen. As hard as I worked to raise the fucking money, I wasn't going to throw it away bailing people out of jail.

I figured we'd send them out on one of the boats with some hookers and booze. We'd keep two boats searching, and Billy and I would man the glass house. Mike freaked out. "Fuck those guys. We're here to do a job. Who in the hell needs a night off from sitting on your ass waiting!"

He had a point, so we settled on a night off at the little yacht club at Cape Ann Marina. We'd send out all the boats, and Billy and I would stay by the radios. Mike still didn't love the idea, but I guarantee you he would never miss a good party.

It was a Tuesday night, but the party scene on the North Shore was in full swing. Every night was the Fourth of July in midsummer on the New England shore. The little yacht club was bouncing with live music and dancing, endless booze, and unattached women. I had been instructed to watch over the flock and check in regularly—it wasn't so much a promotion as an acknowledgment that I was least likely to do something stupid.

I had not been instructed, however, to sit alone in the corner and drown myself in sobriety. I had been drinking in clubs since I was fifteen years old. I knew how to have a good time without totally abandoning my self-control.

I hadn't been there long when I met a young woman. Her name was Jeanette, and she was a nurse at a local hospital. She was tall and fit, with hair the color of mahogany, and a faintly freckled complexion that brought it all together with stunning effect. After a few dances, I got drinks, and we sat down to talk. Once it was established that we were both unattached, the conversation came easily. Others, of course, were lining up for a dance, but Jeanette politely declined. The sparks were flying.

I have never been the kind of guy who could walk into a bar and connect with a woman. I was shy and self-conscious, with a fear of rejection that rendered the slightest overture a life-altering trauma. Small talk, especially small talk with women, had never been one of my trademarks. But on that night I was somebody else—part of a traveling road crew working on the phone lines. That guy had somehow managed to meet an interesting and attractive woman.

I'll take it from here.

Somewhere between *Third Rate Romance* and *Love Will Keep Us Together*, I knew Jeanette was someone I wanted to know better—much better. And what was more astounding, I sensed she had similar feelings. True to my word, I reluctantly excused myself and regularly dropped a dime (a quarter actually) to check in with the glass house. My perfunctory conversations with Billy Russell hardly varied.

"How's the party?"

"Good. Anything happening there?"

"Nope, all quiet."

"Okay, talk to you later."

Though no one else on the crew seemed to be having the luck I was enjoying, everyone was having a good time. The music was great, the booze was plentiful, and the laughter was back. Some of the guys were talking about taking rooms at the marina and passing out on an actual bed. I was beginning to think I might like to do the same, perhaps even passing out with the lovely Jeanette. A little bit of slow dancing toward the end of the evening had whipped the old hormones into a fever pitch.

Around one am, I excused myself once again and headed to the pay phone to make what I hoped would be the final call of the night. Billy Russell answered as usual.

"Hey, Billy," I said. "Everything okay?"

"No," he answered.

"No?" It took a second to register. "Do we need to be there?"

"Yes. Now!" Click.

Ralph Armendariz

We keep thinking, "Maybe they're out here, but we just can't see them and they can't see us." All we can do is wait.

So I'm sitting there, and all of a sudden Toto comes up to me and says, "I see something coming towards us."

And I said, "Well, fuck, get inside! Get everybody inside!" And so we're all inside just kind of looking out the door, and I see something bouncing on the waves. Whatever it was, their lights were turned off, and it was coming towards us. And then it swings right in front of our boat a little ways off, and I hear, "Ralph! Ralph!"

It was Jimmy! I yelled, "Hey man, am I glad to see you guys. I didn't think you were coming."

There wasn't a lot of time for talking. They pulled that boat alongside, and I told the Colombians, "Start pulling that shit out."

So we did. We started throwing it out and loading his boat. We loaded her to the gills. Jimmy gave me a two-way radio, and told me, "Look, I think there's another boat coming out tonight."

And I said, "Okay. When you come back tomorrow, we need water, we need food, and we need cigarettes. And bring me a bottle of Jack Daniels!"

I kicked the anthill and set off a goat fuck that swept through the club in a wave of confusion. Chairs toppled, drinks spilled, bodies lurched. But somehow, we got out of there standing.

When I made my excuses to the disappointed Jeanette, citing trouble somewhere up the phone lines, she penned her name and number on a napkin. I tucked it safely away. A kiss goodnight was all we shared. But it was an extremely promising kiss.

We had arrived in two rental cars. We left in the same two. There ends the similarity between events. We departed in a hail of squealing tires and flying gravel. Speed limits shuddered at our approach as we raced down the shore like a moonshiners' caravan. Steve Andrade drove one car with half the crew. Johnny Milliorn drove the other with Mike and me and the rest of the guys.

I was riding shotgun and explained to Johnny that no mention had been made of the pot being on fire. Maybe dying in a fiery crash or getting arrested along the way wasn't the best idea. He slowed down. Mike, who had remained calm and steady through eight nights of waiting, had erupted into full rant. As mellow of a stoner as he was, he was that bad of a drunk. He didn't want the night off in the first place. And he was not happy to be caught unawares.

We were first to reach the glass house, announcing our arrival like Shriners at a hotel bar. Jack and Billy did their best to quiet everything down. Mike continued to bellow as we set up the dock and cable—a task we had been able to accomplish in less than five minutes. Fifteen minutes later, we were still fumbling around in the ocean as Dave Thomas and Scott Emlong waited patiently aboard the fully loaded *Just A Habit*. The sobering effect of the cool water began to clear my head as we finally set to work loading the first net and attaching it to the hook.

We signaled with our penlight. No response. We signaled again. The net failed to budge. What's going on up there? Our little dock was piled high with pot, and Mike Halliday was coming to a boil. Still far removed from anything approaching a clear head, he marched to the top.

Jack Stricklin

Jimmy Chagra was the one who found the boat. He was with Dave Thomas and Scott Emlong on *Just A Habit*. He loaded up and came back to get the crew and the rest of the boats. When we all met back at the glass house, you could see Peter's neck shrivel up. I mean he was horrified that this was actually happening. *Well, no shit it's happening. It's supposed to happen!* He couldn't get out of there fast enough.

And right after he left, Steve Andrade got stopped by a cop. We heard it on the scanner, and I'm thinking, "We haven't even started this motherfucker and half the crew's going to jail."

I give Steve credit for this—he could talk that telephone talk. "We're here working on the phone lines," he told the cop. "We've been partying, but we just got a call from dispatch. I guess we were in too much of a hurry."

The cop ran Steve's license, and it came back clean, so he said, "Okay, you can go. Be careful." That would never happen today. We got lucky.

So they finally get there, and here comes Mike. I think he was frustrated at himself, and he had to vent somewhere, so he went after Steve Andrade for getting stopped by the cops. Next thing you know, they're shoving each other and Mike coldcocked him. It was Johnny Milliorn who stepped in between them. But for a minute, things got really loud. We couldn't have got off to a worse start if we turned ourselves in.

As we waited below on the dock, tuned into the lightning round of "Loud & Stupid," we all wanted to jump aboard *Just A Habit* and head right back out to sea. How do you forget you've got a boat full of pot in your backyard? *Hello. Remember that smuggle we came to do*?

It took awhile, but everyone's attention finally turned to the job in front of us. Dave and Scott continued to unload the boat handing bales up to the platform where Buzzy Harrison and I filled the nets, attached the hook, and gave the signal. Up they went, five bales to a load—each weighing forty to fifty pounds.

The load came in tightly wrapped bricks stuffed in burlap sacks. A pungent, earthy smell overwhelmed the ocean breeze and covered us all with a fine dust. If there was a drug-sniffing police dog within a mile or two, it was probably barking to beat the band.

Shortly, Mike returned to the dock in a state of relative calm. He wordlessly fit himself to the chain and fell into rhythm. The unsteady little dock rolled with the tide. But it held its own. The pulley, on the other hand, performed heroically. *Just a Habit* was emptied, and *Red Leg* was on the way in with more.

Ralph Armendariz

By now it's getting pretty late. The sun would be coming up soon. And we are not going to be inside international waters when the sun comes up. We knew how long it would take us to get out, and we were getting close to that time limit. No other boat had shown up.

All of a sudden, the radio comes on and says, "Hey, Ralph, how far are you from the Rodeo?" *What? That's the same name as that little town I stayed in Colombia.* I didn't answer. And then they came back again, "Ralph, come on. How far are you from the Rodeo?" I still didn't answer. I didn't know who the fuck was talking to me. And it was a CB radio—it could have been anybody.

Then all of a sudden, he said, "This is Brad. Tell me how far you are from the Rodeo." First of all, I was freaked out that he mentioned the name Rodeo. I found out later he was saying "Rotary." I didn't even know what that was. So he says, "Can you give me a flash of your light? I need to see where you're at. Just give me one flash."

I said, "I'm gonna give you a quick one, so be looking." And then I asked the Captain, "What direction should he be looking in? And I think he said northeast. So I told Doug to look northeast. And boom—we turned on our lights, kept them on for two, three, four, five seconds, boom, turned it off. Then Brad came back on. He says, "I got it. I'm coming."

I said, "Well, haul ass, man."

By that time, we're loading. The back of his boat was a mountain of bales. Everybody was working as fast as they could go so we could get out of there.

Brad Dexter

The night everybody else went out partying, we went out like always. But it was a weird night—just different. We couldn't get anybody on the radios. We never heard from the other boats—nothing. I guess about midnight we decided to head in and maybe catch the tail end of the party. The little club was right there at the Cape Ann Marina—that's where we kept the boat.

We probably got to the bar around one am. None of the guys were there—they were gone, and they sure hadn't gone to bed. The bartender told us they all ran out in a big hurry. Well, that could only mean one thing. We jumped right back on the boat and headed out to The Rotary. The harbor was a no-wake zone, five mile-an-hour speed limit. We were probably doing close to twenty.

By the time we found the trawler, I knew it was too late to make it back in before the sun came up. But I wasn't sure we were ever going to find it again, so I decided the best thing to do was load up and head in. If they couldn't get us offloaded, we'd hang out on the ocean all day and wait for it to get dark.

When we got to the glass house, they were finishing up with *Just A Habit* so I climbed up the hill to talk to Jack. Just like I thought, he said we were done for the night. So we headed back out to the ocean with pot piled four bales high on our back deck.

❀ ❀ ❀

The offload passed in a blur as bale after bale was lifted to the top and carried to the waiting step vans. Between the alcohol and the adrenaline, there hadn't been a lot of time to obsess over the risk. We mindlessly worked our way through the first boatload and were ready for more. But no more pot would be offloaded that night. The dawn had arrived, and we had survived our drunken encounter to fight another day.

At the top, Billy Russell was in full accounting mode, tallying the take as best he could. He would eventually weigh and grade every pound, but for now a rough estimate would have to do. I was curious, but I knew enough to stay out of his kitchen while he was trying to cook. Our job was to vacate the premises as quickly and quietly as possible.

On the ride home, I thought about how my life had changed in just a few short weeks. I realized that in this singular moment in time, I was exactly where I wanted my life to be, doing what I wanted to do. The adrenaline high was like nothing I had ever experienced.

I was a happy guy as my thoughts turned to the lovely Jeanette. Business would come first, but the end was now in sight. There would be plenty of time to get reacquainted. As my hand instinctively reached for my pocket to retrieve her phone number, it suddenly hit me that the promise of Jeanette would remain forever unfulfilled. The ocean had turned my napkin into a soggy lump of sorrow.

DAY TWO

Ralph Armendariz

Our deck is full of grass. So we get the hoses and wash it off, get all the bales put away, shut the hatches. Then we spend the day just sitting around in international waters. The Colombians are asleep. Everybody's indoors. Nobody's sleeping outside. If anybody sees those guys, they're gonna know they're not fisherman.

I'm sitting there drinking coffee, and I'm looking out at the ocean. I've been up all night, but I'm still so hyper. All of a sudden, I hear motors. I'm just listening, listening—then I look out the open door. I don't know how many yards away, but close enough to see its markings, there's a Coast Guard cutter. I see it pass the door. I see them looking at the boat. I mean they're far enough away where I can't see faces, but I can see bodies, figures pass by. And then, at the end of the boat, there's a big old machine gun—50 caliber.

I wait a while. Then I get up and go up to the door. I just stick my head out a little bit, and the cutter keeps on going, doesn't stop. It was probably just a routine patrol, but they were checking us out pretty good. We'd been through so much to get ourselves across the ocean. We were so close to pulling it off. But I didn't feel happy or satisfied—I was kind of scared, honestly. What surprised me the most was that everybody else on the boat felt the same way.

I woke up after a few hours of sleep and began to count the places on my body that didn't ache. I was not alone. The Barracks came alive to the groaning realization that a late night of serious drinking topped off by an early morning of heavy lifting was not something your body would tolerate without protest. But the time for complaining was over. We were in full business mode.

There was still about a 1,000 pounds of pot inside the glass house, and it had to be out of there pronto. We didn't exactly know what to make of our nosy neighbor, but the fact that he was currently in the employ of the U.S. Attorney's Office was much discussed. It wouldn't do for him to drop by with a half-ton of extremely fragrant pot in the house.

I rode in the car with Johnny Milliorn and Mike Halliday, while one of the crew followed in the step van. When we arrived at the glass house, Jack and Billy were busy moving pieces around the board, but they stopped down long enough to give us an update. To our surprise, we learned they had pegged the night's haul at around 8,000 pounds. John Hughes from Atlanta had received all but the 1,000 pounds that remained in the house. His crew was already on the road headed home.

No matter what happened from here on, that 7,000 thousand pounds would bring in enough money to pay the Colombians and wipe the slate with investors. We were out of the red and going for the gold.

BILLY RUSSELL

The concept of distribution was something I played a big part developing. Of course Jack had to co-sign it, but he had a way of listening to you, and then it became his plan. Which was good because Jack had enough on his plate trying to raise money and keep everybody happy. He knew what needed to be done, and he knew I would get it done. It was a very intense period of time. I was definitely afraid that this thing would just come apart at the seams, and we would all get arrested and spend the rest of our lives in a deep, dark dungeon somewhere. So I took nothing for granted.

We had guys assigned to drive the step vans from the glass house, guys to drive the U-Hauls, guys to offload at the staging houses. We rented four satellite locations and determined how much each could hold and which clients would use them to pick up their loads, and when.

The idea was to have that stuff go out of the glass house into the secondary house, then loaded and gone. No sitting around. No lingering. The faster we got it spread out to the various clients, the more chances we had of success because it would be harder to corral.

John Hughes from Atlanta was our biggest customer. We wanted to get him out of there first with as much as we could. We had Italian clients from New York. We counted on them for quick money so we'd take care of them early. Then we'd fill up our Pittsburgh client. Anything going to New England would be last—we didn't want our pot in the area while we were still active.

Brad Dexter

Just a Habit needed to load up with food and water to take out to the trawler. So we moved the pot from the back deck of *Red Leg* and onto *Priscilla III*, then we headed in to refuel.

The marina was probably a mile inside the harbor—no wake, five miles-an-hour. The whole front cabin was filled with pot, and anybody could see we were pretty far down in the bow. And that pot really stunk—you could smell it a mile away. That was probably the scariest part of the whole day. We stayed as far away as we could from other boats and made sure everybody could see our fishing poles. We didn't hang around long. We got our fuel, some food and water, and idled on back out to the ocean to hook up with *Priscilla III,* and take back the rest of our load. Then we headed out to the ocean and disappeared for a while.

Neither one of us got much sleep. We had 8,000 pounds on board—the only place to lie down was on the pot. There's a reason they don't make bed sheets out of burlap. I doubt we could have slept anyway. We were first in that night, and the adrenaline was keeping us wide-awake.

RALPH ARMENDARIZ

So second night, we come in. And now I'm getting a call on the radio telling me, "Ralph, can you come in closer to the coast?"

I told them, "I'll come in closer, but I don't wanna see coast lights."

And then a boat pulled up next to us. By that time, I could just yell at him. "How much further?"

He said, "Come a little further. The closer you get, the more boats we'll be able to load."

"Well, okay." So we kept going.

All of a sudden, I see coast lights. I told the captain, "Stop." I said, "That's it. This is as far as I'm coming in, man."

And we loaded him right there. The sea was a little rough—we even dropped a bale in the ocean. We had a hell of a time fishing it out, but we got it. I knew the Coast Guard was in the area, and we didn't need a bale of marijuana floating around.

So that boat takes off and here comes another one. This time, there's a woman on the boat. We already had all the pot loaded up in a huge pile on deck, and she's out there yelling, "Oh my God, I've never seen so much marijuana in my life!" She was a real talker—the first woman we'd seen in a month. But we were fed up with the whole thing. The Colombians were fed up. I was fed up. We just wanted to get it over with. And we didn't find it exciting. We didn't find it neat. And we didn't want to talk about it. I wanted to get out of there as soon as possible because I could see the coast lights. That's what was bothering me.

By ten pm, we were set up and ready to go. Mike Halliday, Buzzy Harrison, and I were down on the dock with Brad Dexter and Dan Cacy, who had already tied up alongside in the *Red Leg*, the second of three cabin cruisers that would ferry the pot ashore. We had one man stationed along the path to discourage the neighbor from popping in for cocktails. The rest of the crew stood by at the top. The moon was full, the tide was rolling in, and it was time to go to work.

Or it would have been if not for the scuba class preparing for their night dive in the middle of our little cove. Once more we could only sit and wait as the divers were staged from the small parking lot about a hundred yards across the cove. We followed their lights as they submerged. Then Mike and I climbed quietly up to the platform and prepared the net as bales were handed in our direction. Into the net, onto the hook, up to the top, load the second net, repeat. We kept the cable humming until the divers began to resurface, then it was all stop.

On one of the previous nights, we had dispatched a car to the parking lot in order to assess our exposure and determine the range of hi-beam headlights. The results were inconclusive. We weren't exactly invisible, but you would have to be looking closely to notice anything unusual. A diver popping up in the middle of the cove, however, was a threat we never anticipated.

At that moment in time, the adrenaline level at Folly Cove was in the red. The divers were sky high, and we were amped nearly to the point of illumination, though all we could do was wait and listen as they stowed their gear and relived every bubbling breath. Finally, the celebration faded to an echo as they headed down the highway, and we got back to the business of heavy lifting.

We finished off *Red Leg* and received *Priscilla III*. In what Peter Kruschewski might describe as a mutinous display of insubordination, his landing crew abandoned the Stevens Point house and headed to the glass house to pitch in. They were sorely needed. As hard as we were working on the dock, the guys at the top were working even harder, pulling 300 pounds at a time up the steep incline, then loading the vans. They rotated in and out, resting every five or six pulls before attaching themselves once again to the rope. There had to be at least a dozen guys up there, but you never would have known. The only sound we heard was the hum of the cable and the roar of the surf.

Though we could have used more hands down below, there was simply no place to put them. With two of us on the platform, two on the dock, and two in the boat, we were at full capacity. Another body would have been one too many. The pot was stacked four bales high and spread over most of the dock. We whittled it down to six bales at a time until the boat was empty. A full one would be right in its wake.

We worked in silent syncopation, loading those bales and hauling that rope. Nobody was complaining now—there was little energy for negative thoughts. If you looked beyond the bale that was in front of your eyes, you'd fall out of rhythm. We knew exactly how much time would elapse before the guys at the top were ready for another go, and we adjusted our pace accordingly.

It is an interesting thing about awareness. Seek it passively, and you'll probably fall asleep. But put a body in motion, and your mind is set free from the passage of time as you enter a state of focus that is absolute. I imagine that's the genesis of PTSD—an event so intense it lives forever in your mind.

Though our adventure pales in comparison to the life and death pressure of war, it is nevertheless etched with the same kind of clarity. Forty years after the fact, I can still hear the soundtrack of the oncoming tide mixed with the low rumble of an idling engine and the high-pitched hum of the cable. I can still smell the pot—loamy and pungent, mingling with the scent of the sea and the hot breath of burning diesel. I remember welcoming the full moon tide as it lifted us nearly to the level of the platform. And I remember my own feverish compulsion to get those itchy bales off the dock and out of my life as fast as was humanly possible. It wasn't courage that moved that pot. It was fear, which was all the motivation any of us would ever need.

At around two am, with the tide going out, a police car unexpectedly pulled into the little parking lot across the inlet and stopped with its lights shining on Folly Cove. We knew the local police enforced a diving curfew, and we knew the little parking lot overlooking the cove was a popular spot for a little late-night lust. But when that policeman got out of his patrol car and began to scan the cove with his spotlight, all we knew for certain was the cold shiver of dread.

We froze in place, terrified of making the slightest movement. The way sound traveled across that cove, a sudden fart could be our undoing. Up top, all ears tuned to the scanners, while we stood frozen in time, contemplating the merits of an immediate exit strategy. My mind was in overdrive, commanding me to do anything but remain in place. I was experiencing fear, not as an emotion, but as a physical assault on every cell in my system. The instinct of panic was gaining momentum by the heartbeat. But we stood firm and held to our stillness as a matter of faith— in each other and in whatever higher power we chose to invoke.

After what seemed a lifetime but was probably closer to five minutes, the spotlight relinquished its hold on our collective sphincter, and the cop went on his way. But our energy had been spent. The synchronized rhythm of our earlier effort was replaced by the pain and sweat of an endlessly grueling job.

Somehow we kept going, wondering if it would ever end. We had no idea how much pot we had sent up the cable. But if the load was anywhere near the predicted 35,000 pounds, we had to be getting close. Around 4:30 in the morning, word came down that we were done for now. The trawler still had more to give. We, on the other hand, had nothing left.

SEEDS & STEMS

If in the entire history of air mattresses, one had ever been as comfortable as the one on which I passed out that morning, I would consider it a sacred relic. We slept like the dead and awoke to the groaning reality of one more night in the breech.

Happy customers were on their way to market. Three large U-Hauls were already out of the area headed toward safe houses near Pittsburgh, New York, and Atlanta. The fourth was just outside our front door with a partial load. For the moment, there was nothing much to do but wait, something at which I was becoming quite accomplished.

When we got to the glass house late in the afternoon, Scott Emlong was fine-tuning his perfect tan on the little dock below while Jack Stricklin, Billy Russell, and Jimmy Chagra were conducting a roundtable on the subject of Peter Kruschewski's gonads. Last night we had offloaded six boats—a rough estimate of 37,000 pounds, bringing the total somewhere around 45,000 pounds. Not a single ounce had been offloaded anywhere in the vicinity of Peter Kruschewski.

The plan had been to spread the offload in order to hasten the process and minimize the risk. But Peter and risk were proving to be mutually exclusive. Jimmy and Peter argued loudly, with Jack and Billy occasionally piling on. We might have actually been finished by now had Peter Kruschewski come anywhere close to holding up his end. He could easily have moved a few thousand pounds on his little boat. And his crew was chomping at the bit to get involved. But Peter felt the enterprise was best served by hovering at a safe distance to oversee the boat crews. He was our man in the water, safely directing boats that required neither oversight nor direction.

"Besides," he told everyone, "the Stevens Point House isn't as private as I thought it was...and if you hadn't taken my fucking crew it would have been available as a secondary...and I'm the one that put the deal together in the first place. So fuck you."

Glad we could talk it out.

Ralph Armendariz

I saw the Coast Guard Cutter again the next morning. It was definitely checking us out. We still had pot on board, but all we could do was cruise around in international waters and wait for the sun to go down. They had brought out some supplies so we had food and water, but most of the guys were too tired to eat or drink.

I was sitting in the galley with the Colombian captain. He told me that he was supposed to get $25,000 or $30,000. And I said, "I don't know anything about that."

He says, "It's what they told me, and if I don't get it, you're not getting off."

I said, "I'll get off the fucking boat, even if I have to shoot you to get off the fucking boat."

And so we argued pretty heavily. We were gonna come to blows. We were that close. That was why I asked Jimmy to bring out the Jack Daniels. I went and got it and I said, "Come on, let's calm down and have a drink." So we sat there and drank shots of Jack Daniels until we got shit-faced. He loosened up after we got drunk, man. And I just told him, "Look, you're gonna be taken care of. I don't know if Jimmy's bringing money out tonight, but it's gonna work out. You're going to be taken care of."

I knew there wasn't going to be any money. Jimmy told me we were out of money. But the Colombians had a list—a gift list—stereos, radios, guns. And that last night they did bring some out—I don't think there was any guns, but they brought out gifts for all the guys. I didn't really care what it was. I was ready to get off that fucking boat.

The trawler was down to its last 8,000 pounds or so. Only two boats would be sent out that night. All that remained was to top off the final U-Haul and send the last of the pot on its merry way. As darkness descended, we waited quietly on the little dock, unaware of the scene unfolding some twelve miles out to sea.

With Peter Kruschewski in his Formula boat, Jimmy Chagra on the *Red Leg*, and Scott Emlong and Dave Thomas aboard *Just a Habit*, they tied up to the trawler to assess the night's work. It looked like a single boat would be sufficient. And since *Red Leg* had the largest capacity, *Just a Habit* was sent back to the glass house to help with the offload.

The Colombians were anxious to head home so the loading proceeded apace with *Red Leg* filled to the point of overflowing. But a few bales remained. All eyes turned to Peter Kruschewski as he stood in the cockpit of his empty boat and ordered the bales to be dumped in the sea.

I want to believe that despite the nearly twelve miles that separated us, we could clearly hear Jimmy Chagra screaming in Arabic as he let loose a tirade that would have rattled the tomb of the pharaohs. Jimmy may have been loose with money at the blackjack table, but he wasn't about to toss more than $250,000 worth of perfectly good pot into the ocean. According to witnesses, he threatened to castrate Peter Kruschewski if that pot wasn't loaded onto his boat and taken back to Stevens Point. An enraged Jimmy was not something you wanted to fuck with. Peter reluctantly complied. Back at the glass house, we made short work of the remaining load as another four tons were hoisted aloft, loaded into vans and headed for the final staging house.

RALPH ARMENDARIZ

And so the last boat comes out, and we get it loaded up until we couldn't get any more on there, and we still had—I don't know, maybe ten, fifteen bales. The boat that Peter was driving looked like one of those cigarette boats—a fast-ass boat. He didn't want to take the pot, but the Colombians sure as hell weren't going to keep it, and I didn't bring it all that way to throw it in the ocean. He and Jimmy argued about it—Jimmy got really pissed, but in the end they loaded it on Peter's boat, and I came in with it to the house at Steven's Point.

We came in through a dock area. I mean, there were people walking on the damn dock—they were everywhere. The lights were on, and we came in pretty slow. We were close enough to the dock that I could see people moving around. And then the boat came up and ended up just kind of like on a dirt area. It wasn't a beach or anything. It was just a small, little patch of shore.

There were some people there, and they came down and unloaded. I didn't take one bale up. I thought, "I'm not unloading this shit." I stayed there until a van came. They loaded it up and took it away. That's when Peter drove me to the glass house.

Johnny Milliorn was the first one I saw, and he grabbed me and he hugged me and he said, "Damn, Ralph, we thought you were dead meat, man. You took so long to get here, we thought you were lost." He said, "Man, it's good to see you." That's when I knew it was all over, we did it—holy shit we did it!

The first thing I did was I took a shower. All this grass

was in my hair and everywhere else. I probably lost about twenty-five pounds—none of my clothes fit, but I was just happy to be wearing something clean. I went outside and watched them bring up the final bales. Jimmy Chagra showed up, and we stayed there for a little while, and then we left, and we went to a hotel in Boston. We both flew home in the morning.

We did it! We took a bite out of the horizon and swallowed it whole. The official tally would end up a bug's knuckle short of twenty-nine tons of primo Colombian Red. By the time the last of it went humming up that cable, the first of it was already in the market. After three ball-busting nights of high-stress hard labor, we set in motion a clockwork of moving parts that had meshed with cool efficiency. A little more than 58,000 pounds! It may not be a record that stands for long, but it would be an event that stands alone.

I smoked a joint as the sun came up on that final morning at Folly Cove. It was an epic sunrise, the marine layer finally surrendering to the freshening north wind. Even the gulls were laughing as we cleaned up the seeds and stems that had shaken loose across the grounds like a red frost. It could easily have had a street value in the thousands. We bagged it up as best we could, smoking all we wanted and laughing at the prospects of the cash crop of volunteers that would surely emerge next summer.

As I was picking up pot beneath the apple tree, here comes the diminutive Don Ferris, once again strolling down the path with a drink in his hand. Thankfully, most of the crew had already left. But the ground was still littered with the remains of our load, and the peaty aroma of pot clung to the breeze like a puff of heaven. He could not fail to notice. There were easily a few felonies worth of pot lying around. Don bent over and plucked a juicy bud, inhaling its aroma like a fine wine. He smiled and waved a friendly hello. I tendered the joint I had been smoking, and he gratefully accepted.

"Un-fucking believable!" he said. He could hardly stop laughing.

Don Ferris, it seems, had spent the previous three nights on his veranda with a drink in his hand and a pair of hi-powered binoculars at his fingertips. He watched the entire offload go down and chuckled to himself with each passing bale.

"It took me a while to figure out what you guys were doing, but once I did, I couldn't stop laughing. I can't believe you did it here—in the middle of all these people! How much was it anyway?"

"Somewhere around twenty-nine tons," Jack told him.

Don was old money New England and not easily impressed, but that got his full attention.

"This is not really the place to do this kind of thing," he said. "I can show you places up and down the North Shore where you'll have total privacy. You need a large estate, but the only way you're going to be able to lease a place like that is through a local attorney who knows the ropes. Those people won't even talk to you without one."

Don hadn't just come to congratulate us. He came to apply for a job! He wanted in, and by the time he got through telling us all the ways he could help, Jack anointed him our man in Boston. He was a lawyer, a Harvard man, a Kennedy. This was his backyard, and he could open it up to us in ways that would allow bigger and better deals to come. "We'll be back next summer," Jack told him. "Start looking for a place."

Meanwhile, he was invited to take home any of the remaining pot that littered the grounds. So Don joined what was left of the crew and strolled the area with his baggie, filling up on the remains of our unlikely adventure.

Don Ferris would never get his chance to star in the sequel. By next summer, Jack Stricklin and Billy Russell would be doing time for Roswell while many of the guys drifted away in search of smaller game. Everyone knew the unlikely success of Folly Cove would never be duplicated. We had pushed our luck to the limit and been kissed on the lips by the siren of fortuity. There would be no encore. Our heroic little pulley would be plated in gold to reside forever in the attic of forgotten relics.

As to our rickety dock, no one will ever set foot on it again. The locals, Don told us, had laughed at our attempt to fasten the flimsy structure to the side of a cliff. Within hours of the offload, an early nor'easter would send her to sea in small pieces. The neighbors, no doubt, shared a hearty laugh.

And in fact, so did we.

PART III

GLORY DAYS

CROSS COUNTRY

JACK STRICKLIN

Most of the crew went home. For them, it was over. For Billy Russell and me, it was just the beginning. We had no time to stop and think about what we'd done—the celebration would come later. We had twenty-nine tons of pot on the ground, and we had to get it into the market and turn it into cash. We still had a hostage in Colombia, and we wanted to bring him home.

Now, I might have moved twenty-niine tons of pot in a good season—that was over four or five months. Dealing with it all at once was a huge job. Billy Russell and I immediately got on a plane for Atlanta. There was still a lot of moisture in that pot, and we had to turn it, weigh it, and grade it. Thank God for Billy. He worked his ass off the whole time we were together. I couldn't have done it without him. We covered three different stash houses around the country, and he accounted for every pound of that load.

The pot was outstanding. There were no complaints about quality. We got $275 a pound, and our customers were happy to pay it. Of course, most of the big ones got three-to-one in product, so it would end up being less than that. But a lot of people got rich, and not a single pound of that load got busted.

Billy Russell

During the Boston deal, I asked Mike and Jack if they would let me have weight so I could make more money than the rates they were paying the crew. I'd already sold quite a bit of merchandise when we were doing the Mexican thing. Jack and Mike were happy to do it. Jack always encouraged his guys to do their own thing. Turning them into buyers was better for everybody. And of course, there was so much pot they didn't know what to do with it all.

I had clients in Minneapolis and a partner who had clients of his own in the Philadelphia area. So I actually had two pretty decent customers. I think I got somewhere around 6,000 pounds. I made about $300,000. In 1975, that was a lot of money. I was pretty enthralled with myself. But I was still up to my ass accounting for all that pot.

I had been promised $25,000 for my participation. When you consider the deal generated somewhere in the neighborhood of $12 million, my share amounted to less than fifty cents a pound. But given that I only made about $6,000 a year at the ad agency, it was a staggering amount, more money than I had ever made. And it was enough to allow me to kick back and spend my days riding dirt bikes, drinking beer, and pursuing an agenda that had little or nothing to do with actual work. But the Boston deal wasn't quite over for me.

I didn't see much of Jack Stricklin or Billy Russell immediately after Boston. They followed the pot. Jack and Mike owned most of the distribution. And Billy Russell was so critical to the operation that he would have to delegate the distribution of his own piece of the load. He offered me the chance to drive a ton of pot from Atlanta to Minneapolis at the going rate of $5 a pound—another $10,000 for less than twenty-four hours work. *Hell, yes.*

Though driving a load doesn't quite match the hair-on-fire intensity of the initial smuggle, it exposes you to greater risk. Your best chance of being busted comes at the pick-up and delivery points. You are at the mercy of your customers on both ends of the chain. If they brought heat, that's when you'd feel it. They, of course, are equally paranoid about the heat you might be bringing.

Now don't get me wrong, it doesn't take a man of letters to drive a load of grass. But it is a step up from a mule. You need to know your route, plan your stops, stay awake, and keep both hands on the wheel. Take care of the details, and your chances of success are high. As long as your pickup and delivery points are uncompromised, you almost have to fuck up to get caught.

I flew to Atlanta and met Billy. He had me rent a U-Haul truck. It was a van actually, with a cargo box more or less partitioned from the stubby cab by a flimsy piece of plywood—it was the furthest thing from airtight. The stench of the pot would be with me for most of the drive, but as long as I kept moving it shouldn't be a too big a problem.

Billy made sure I had the phone numbers memorized and nothing incriminating in my possession. He advised me to steer clear of Chicago—the few extra miles it took to go around were well worth the time. And he told me that a little baby powder would help cut the smell.

I was taken to a little place outside Atlanta to receive the load. It was a picturesque southern farmhouse with a sturdy red barn and total privacy. It belonged to John Hughes and his partner, and like everything they owned, it was pristine. It helped that I had gotten to know them on previous trips with Jack. They were standup guys and totally professional in their approach.

We tallied up and loaded in short order. Before attaching the padlock and throwing away the keys, I cut open two large containers of baby powder and tossed them on top. I figured if one would mask the smell, two might obliterate it. I hit the road in the late afternoon.

It was the golden hour. The setting sun was streaking through the towering pines as the shadows stretched across the highway. I motored along in the remnants of rush-hour traffic, on my way to Minneapolis with a ton of pot. I could hardly keep from laughing out loud as I pegged the needle at a conservative sixty miles—enough over the fifty-five mile speed limit to keep from totally pissing off other drivers, but not so much as to attract the attention of law enforcement. All I had to do was keep the rubber side down and stay awake. My confidence was beginning to soar.

After a few miles, I began to notice my visibility becoming impaired. *What did that last road sign say? Where did that car come from?* I found myself squinting at the road ahead. Maybe the shadows were playing tricks. Maybe I was having an acid flashback. Or maybe, just maybe it was the fact that the inside of my cab had broken out in a force-5 blizzard of baby powder!

I rolled down my window to release a cloud. I cleaned my glasses and waved my hand in front of my face. I turned the fan up to high. Nothing helped. I cursed Ford Motor Company for not putting windshield wipers on the inside and pushed on like an Iditarod musher. I can only imagine what passing motorists must have thought.

Look Mommy, that man is driving a snow-globe!

Billy Russell

> Another thing I did in return for the product I received was collect the money. I was part of the inner circle by then. Jimmy Chagra, Peter Kruschewski, and Jack Stricklin said, "We're gonna get Billy to keep books." They didn't trust each other. I trusted Mike and Jack, but I didn't trust the other two guys. So I kept the books, and that meant I had to see all the money.
>
> I collected at least $12 million, most of it in a Learjet from Caesar's Palace. We had clients up and down the East Coast and as far west as Minnesota. When they collected

enough cash, I would make a loop with the Lear and come back heavy—$1 to $2 million dollars.

Wherever I flew, I was always in a suit and tie. The Learjet would land on the executive ramp, and I would call a taxicab. I would never use one that was waiting there. Never. I'd have the cab take me to an undisclosed location and then make a phone call to get picked up by the client. I didn't want them to know anything about the Learjet because sometimes I had to leave it on the ramp with the pilots and as much as a $1 millon on board. They had a gun.

The key to the whole thing is that you can't let your mouth rattle off too much information about where you were, where you're going, and when you're going. When I would fly out of Las Vegas, I would tell the pilots, "Draw a flight plan to Reno." And after we got up in the air en route to Reno, I would say, "Okay, now take me to Atlanta.", So they would change the flight plan in mid-air. I knew what was legal and what was illegal in terms of flight regulations.

When we flew back to Las Vegas, Ceasar's Palace would meet me at the plane with the limo. They treated me like a potentate—everything was on the house. I would have these three big suitcases filled with money—mostly $20 bills, a serious weight. We loaded it onto the limo, and went to the hotel.

The money all went through the cage at Caesar's Palace and came back in nice crisp hundred dollar bills.

I ended up doing a lot of traveling with Jack. He rarely went anywhere alone. After my performance in Boston, I seemed to have moved a few rungs up the ladder. Our business mostly consisted of meeting with clients, arranging for the transfer of money and product, and staying out of El Paso where the local

DEA was scratching their heads at the number of brand new cars they were suddenly following.

The next load I drove for Billy Russell happened a few weeks later—another ton, another $10,000. Once again, I picked it up in Atlanta, but this time I would deliver it just outside of Philadelphia. And this time I would be pulling a trailer, so there would be no repeat of the baby powder blizzard! I won't say that on only my second delivery the job of pulling a ton of pot cross-country had become routine. But the fact that I had done it once took a little edge off the anxiety. What made this deal a little more complicated was that I would be returning with $100,000 in cash.

I successfully delivered the load to Allentown, Pennsylvania, and headed for a nearby regional airport to catch a flight to Philadelphia and my connection home. I packed the money carefully in large self-addressed manila envelopes and added plenty of postage. Airport security was cursory in those days, and they didn't have the authority to open mail. But the envelopes were way too bulky to fit in my briefcase, so they had to go in my carry-on. But when I boarded the small commuter plane, I was told there was no room for my carry-on. It would have to be checked. I was assured it would be waiting when I landed in Philadelphia.

"In Delta Airlines We Trust." I was hardly comforted by the thought.

As we began to taxi away from the terminal, I happened to look out my window and was surprised—no, horrified—to see my lonesome carry-on sitting on the tarmac. "Wait a minute. There's been a huge mistake. Turn this motherfucker around!"

But of course I couldn't say any of that. I could only sit through the thirty-minute flight and grind my molars to a fine dust. The instant we hit the gate in Philadelphia, I sprinted to the first Delta agent I saw and began to rant like a runaway lunatic.

I berated that poor woman with everything I had. She would feel my pain and she would, by god, move her ass to make it right!

I have to say that the particular Delta agent I verbally assaulted was likely destined for sainthood. She would have been justified to shoot me in self-defense. But she deflected my anger like a Jedi Knight. It was as if she laid me down and rubbed by belly.

"It's already en route," she reported. "It will be on the ground in fifteen minutes, and you'll make your connection in plenty of time. Meanwhile, why don't you allow Delta Airlines to buy you a drink?"

Man plans and God laughs.

WAGES OF SIN

Jack called me one morning not long after I returned from Philadelphia and told me to get ready to travel.

"What time do I need to be at the airport?"

"Whenever you get there, brother. We're taking the Learjet."

It had been suggested that I bring my party clothes, which in the '70s implied a leisure suit over a boldly printed high-collared silk shirt that opened to your navel. Gold chains were essential, though I was a bit behind in my acquisition of the appropriate weight and carat. Chest hair would have been the next best thing, but even there I was lacking. I made up for it with a stylish shag haircut and a dangerously drooping mustache. I was rockin' the latest look, though there's not a doubt in my mind that the fashion tragedy of the '70s was the result of an acid trip gone horribly wrong.

Jack Stricklin, Billy Russell, and I checked into the penthouse suite of the recently completed Peachtree Hyatt Regency in downtown Atlanta. Mike Halliday would fly in later that day with Johnny Milliorn. Jimmy Chagra elected to confine his celebration to the casinos of Las Vegas, where he and Ralph Armendariz were holding a party of their own.

John Hughes and his partner were on hand to host the gala. John took care of the entertainment. Leave it to the gay guy to get the hookers. His taste in everything was beyond impeccable—he showed an equally discriminating eye in the selection of escorts. These were "Goddesses of Negotiable Affection"—gorgeous and sophisticated women you would be proud to have on your arm. And beneath those breathtakingly hot exteriors were enough street smarts to appreciate the nature of our business and the origins of our cash. They were impressed. And so were we.

We ate in the finest restaurants, drank rare and expensive wine, and shopped at all the hottest establishments. We paid them for a night and ended up spending three days together, sharing every kind of recreational drug known to man. By the second night, the girls had not only contributed their own stash to the festivities, they brought along a few new friends to join the fun.

As far as the hotel was concerned, in less than twenty-four hours we had evolved from *Who are these yahoos?* to *Is there anything else we can do for you, sir?* By the second night, the manager was calling us to make sure *they* weren't making too much noise. We wallpapered the Hyatt in hundred dollar bills,

L to R: Donna and Jack Stricklin, Marsha and Ralph Armendariz, Joe Annie and Lee Chagra celebrating in Las Vegas shortly after Boston.

tipping like the rock stars we thought we were. The great Sammy Davis Jr. said it best when a friend asked if he had change for a twenty: "A twenty *is* change, babe."

The best restaurants served us wine we couldn't pronounce and food you could hardly find on the plate. The trendiest clubs opened their arms and brought out more bubbly than a North Dallas wedding. And what we couldn't spend, we'd just give away.

Our limousine driver was an engaging and ambitious young black man named Dan. He spoke with the zeal of the freshly converted as he described the potential of the limo service he hoped to one day own and operate. No one was the least bit surprised when Jack Stricklin announced on our way out of town that he was now part owner of an Atlanta limousine service.

The party was a display of excess unseen since the Roman Empire. But beyond the debauchery, we enjoyed a singular moment in time with like-minded women who came to us as hookers and departed as friends. We had shared no past nor anticipated any future. We had only the now and within it we found a similarity of spirit that was the perfect chemistry for an indelible party.

Atlanta marked the end of our landmark summer, but the celebration continued in an unabated spending spree that fortified the economy of El Paso. Everyone who invested a dollar got three in return. Jack Stricklin might as well have ridden around town in a chariot. He could easily have been elected mayor.

Me, I bought a new jeep and a bigger dirt bike and did some traveling just for fun. Billy Russell took his family on a first-class vacation and spoiled his children to within an inch of their lives. Jimmy Chagra spent all his time gambling in Las Vegas. And Mike Halliday fell in love, lavishing his new girlfriend with treasures and trinkets. He had met Karen II and taken the old thunderbolt right through the heart. He appeared to be down for the count.

It was all a blur, frankly. Though I can recall with surprising clarity the details of my days on the North Shore, I remember very little about the disposal of my cash. But I remember how Jack Stricklin disposed of his. In fact, everyone who came within spitting distance of Jack can tell you how he chose to commemorate the event.

Jack and his wife Donna were remodeling their home in the Upper Valley. It was a sprawling two-story adobe ranch surrounded by fields of sweet onions and hot peppers. Ironically, it was just across the road from the Holt place where he had smoked his first joint.

The home was protected from prying eyes by a newly erected eight-foot wall, which contained a menagerie of wildlife that included dogs, cats, and passive-aggressive peacocks. Money was no object. The Stricklins were hip deep in contractors lining up to collect their fees in cash.

The interior was opened up in the Santa Fe style. The kitchen was doubled in size and modernized with the most expensive appliances. They added a nursery fit for a prince. And of course, one could hardly make do with the old furniture.

It was shaping up to be the perfect showplace but for one amendable flaw. El Paso summers are hotter than the devil's armpits. And nothing takes the edge off a blistering day like a nice swimming pool. It is fair to say that most of the decorating decisions were willingly left to Donna. But for some reason, Jack felt the need to personally see to the aesthetics of the swimming pool.

With a bravado that would define his five-year reign as one of the border's preeminent pot smugglers, Jack Stricklin commissioned the sacred mosaic of a seven-foot marijuana leaf to be embedded in the bottom of his swimming pool. It was exquisitely rendered in colorful Italian tile and elegant in its simplicity as it sparkled beneath the shimmering blue water, screaming "Fuck You!" in a skyward direction.

As coincidence would have it, that was precisely the direction in which you would regularly find the DEA, dipping their wings as they repeatedly buzzed The Leaf on a daily schedule. As if they weren't already at his heels, there stood a graphic reminder that bringing Jack Stricklin to ground had arisen to the very top of their to-do list. He might as well have had The Leaf embedded on his forehead.

THE DARK SIDE

It could be argued that Folly Cove was the fulcrum on which the business of marijuana pivoted to the dark side. After 1975, the Mexican and Colombian cartels were awakening to the potential of America's appetite for drugs and began to mark their turf in blood. They vigorously pushed the white—cocaine, much easier to distribute and far more profitable. Oh, and if it wouldn't be too much trouble—or even if it would—they would prefer to be partially paid in guns, lots of guns.

When Jack Stricklin and Billy Russell were sent to La Tuna in early 1976, I was left to work with Mike Halliday and Jimmy Chagra. There was no question that Jimmy was now in charge. He demonstrated it daily by issuing bold proclamations about all the money we would make, then swan diving nose-first into an anthill of cocaine. Jimmy was wired to fail. For him, it was all about greed, power, and conspicuous consumption. He was crooked as a corkscrew, ignoring the odds and casting the dice without conscience.

We did manage to bring in a couple of loads of Mexican. But the pot was mediocre and the profit meager. Colombia was where the money was. Colombia was where Jimmy had established a multi-million dollar connection. And Colombia was where he needed to be. But Jimmy refused to go, sending others instead to do his bidding.

Jimmy and Mike argued long and loud over the merits of

having an actual plan. Object and invective were hurled with equal abandon as they explored the depths of their mutual dislike. I spent my days ducking and dodging between a coked-up gambler and a high-octane bottle rocket. There would be no winner. Jimmy would tell you that he fired Mike. Mike would argue that he quit. I would simply say that Jimmy was a piranha. Mike was a snack.

With Mike and Jimmy going their separate ways, I knew it was time to exit stage left. Mike had a new Karen to support. After the windfall of Boston, she had grown accustomed to excess. So he started over, intent on recapturing past glories. I could have continued to work for Jimmy, but I knew how that would end. I may have been broke, but I was a long way from suicidal. I had given it a couple of years and had no regrets. The gathering storm that was about to make landfall would elevate the risk far beyond anything I was willing to accept.

The truth is, I was never really cut out for the life. To me it was a grand adventure. I believed in the righteousness of the

Kermit Schweidel on visiting day at La Tuna FCI with Billy Russell and Jack Stricklin, 1976.

rebellion, but cocaine would ruin the pot business, and running guns to a South American cartel could seriously derail your future. Sometime around the middle of 1977, I elected to retire undefeated and return to a society where trading guns for drugs in a third-world country was best left to the government.

True to his character, Jimmy Chagra remained a walking calamity. He lost a load of Colombian and a crew of eight in Ardmore, Oklahoma. He lost a pilot in Colombia. And gambled away every dollar he made in the Boston deal. But to Jimmy, a losing streak only meant he was one step closer to a winning streak. Say this for the man: he had some stones.

Jimmy Chagra made his millions off the coast of Florida in the late '70s, where the international cocaine and marijuana traffic was concentrated in a seagoing snarl of historic proportion. He found himself in Florida on the payroll of the last smuggler on earth who would be kind enough or stupid enough to give him a job. It was not Jimmy's load. It was not Jimmy's deal. He was strictly a hired hand, trying to make enough money to set up a score of his own.

One day Jimmy headed out to sea in search of the load he had been contracted to land. He never found the boat he was looking for. But he found boatloads of product begging to be brought ashore. Florida's international cocaine and marijuana traffic was piling up off the coast. So Jimmy Chagra got into a boat, found himself a load and convinced the Colombians that he was their savior. Ultimately, his powers of persuasion netted enough cocaine and marijuana to make him a millionaire many times over.

Jimmy and his new wife Liz moved to Las Vegas and commissioned a mansion of marble and mirrors. He would gamble his way into folklore, overshadowing the image of brother Lee and dominating the spotlight. Jimmy owned the city that Lee had only rented. But it would not be his legendary reputation as a hi-stakes gambler that would etch his place in drug lore.

On the way to making his fortune, Jimmy left behind a trail of unhappy associates who were literally tripping over themselves to give him up. It was immunity with impunity as the government came down on him with everything they could conjure. He was indicted under the kingpin statute and faced a lifetime in prison. Though he believed his fortune put him well beyond the reach of law, he was scheduled to appear before a federal judge with a reputation for being tough on drug dealers. But as far as Jimmy was concerned, Judge John Wood was just a man who thought he could fuck with the King of Las Vegas.

On May 29, 1979, Judge John Wood, known as "Maximum John," was shot in the back with a high-powered hunting rifle just outside his San Antonio condominium. It was the first assassination of a standing United States federal judge in over a hundred years.

Though the Government dedicated countless dollars and limitless manpower to the investigation, the case would remain unsolved for nearly three years. The full weight and measure of the United States government, however, would eventually prevail.

The murder of Judge John Wood and the tragic fate of the Chagra family is a story well told by Gary Cartwright in his book *Dirty Dealing*. It was a dark and complex web of greed and stupidity. The offshoot is that a career criminal named Charles Harrelson was convicted as the shooter and spent the remainder of his life in federal prison. His wife would also be named in the conspiracy.

Once they had custody of the man who pulled the trigger, the Government focused their energy on the one who bought the bullet. It was with great fanfare that they finally indicted Jimmy Chagra for conspiracy to murder Judge Wood. Before his case would come to trial, Jimmy would manage to entangle his closest family.

Joe Chagra passed three polygraph tests, one of them administered by the FBI. Each supported his claim of innocence. As Jimmy's lawyer he was entitled to privilege. The feds thought otherwise. Joe Chagra was no killer and the Government most likely knew it. They were simply looking for leverage.

Threats of a life sentence without parole finally convinced Joe Chagra to cut a deal and testify against Charles Harrelson. But he made it clear that he would not testify against his brother. For his cooperation, Joe would serve the better part of ten years in federal prison, losing his family and his license to practice law in the bargain.

Hardly satisfied with the destruction of his only remaining brother, Jimmy sacrificed his wife Liz on the altar of conspiracy. Despite the fact that she was seven months pregnant at the time, he had insisted that she courier a bundle of cash to Las Vegas. Whether or not she knew the money was a payoff for the murder of Judge Wood is anyone's guess. It was not unusual for her to carry money for Jimmy. She knew its origin, spent it with impunity, and didn't ask a lot of questions. But no one who knew her believed she could be part of the conspiracy to assassinate a standing federal judge. Jimmy, who would have had to incriminate himself to save her, did nothing. The mother of his children would die of cancer while serving time in a federal prison.

True to form, Jimmy Chagra walked between the raindrops. His wife and brother were convicted of conspiracy to murder Judge John Wood, The triggerman and his wife were likewise convicted. But Jimmy Chagra would be acquitted of all charges in connection with the conspiracy to murder Judge Wood. He would, however, be convicted under the Federal Kingpin Statute and be put away for close to twenty years.

BACK TO BOSTON

May of 1980, less than sixty days before the statute of limitations would expire on Folly Cove. Somebody snitched. The DEA came calling with a warrant for my arrest. And suddenly I found myself residing in the federal holding tank at the El Paso County Jail with Billy Russell. Jack Stricklin and the rest of the crew had flown to Boston to surrender to the first circuit, where the indictment had been issued. I knew it would only be a matter of days before I was out on bail, but the reality of several years in prison was beginning to sink in.

I had been living a far different life than the one I found myself being pulled back toward. I was married, pursuing a legitimate career, and more or less law-abiding. But I was the same person who had willingly defied the law, and I did it without shame or regret. The example set by Jack Stricklin, Mike Halliday, Billy Russell, and others was one I was fully committed to follow. I would not cooperate or resist, but place my fate in the hands of a lawyer and take whatever punishment came my way. I did the crime. I would do the time.

Among others named in the forty-two-person indictment were Jimmy Chagra, Jack Stricklin, Mike Halliday, Billy Russell, and Johnny Milliorn. Mike Halliday was a federal fugitive at the time—whereabouts unknown. And Ralph Armendariz was listed as Ralph LNU (Last Name Unknown). Nobody came forward to fill in the blanks.

Scott Emlong and Dan Cacy were the confidential informants. They were caught in the act of landing a load somewhere off the Oregon coast. Though they probably faced less than two years in a minimum-security federal prison, they threw down their *Get-Out-of-Jail-Free card* faster than you can say Jimmy Chagra.

In the autumn of 1980, Jimmy had yet to stand trial for the murder of Judge Wood. He was held in federal custody without bond.

Before he was finally put away, the feds would offer immunity to a slew of drug traffickers and a notorious jailhouse snitch who once occupied a lofty perch on America's ten-most-wanted list. That's how badly they wanted Jimmy Chagra.

On the opening morning of our trial, Jimmy walked into court wearing a stylish new suit and a confident smile. Though he may have been the cornerstone of the case, the charges he faced were of little concern compared to the bucket of crimes he had yet to answer for. Oscar Goodman, his high-profile Las Vegas attorney, had his hands full preparing for the sensational murder trial to come. He simply didn't have time to deal with Boston.

A motion for separation was asked for and granted in exchange for a quick guilty plea and deferred sentencing. Jimmy walked into court, stood quietly before the judge and was ushered out in about five minutes time. The judge couldn't get him out of his courtroom fast enough.

The last time I saw Jimmy Chagra was later that same day in a holding cell just behind the courtroom in the Boston Federal Building. I had been summoned in regard to a court order demanding that Jack Stricklin and I submit to a handwriting analysis so they could prove we had travelled to Atlanta under assumed names. I remember my great surprise as I looked up and saw Jimmy standing there casually leaning on the bars of his cell.

"Hello, brother, got a cigarette?"

"Sure, Jimmy. How are they treating you?" He reached out for a cigarette, but the guard quickly intercepted it and reminded me that contact was strictly verboten. We talked awkwardly for a few minutes. I'm sure the feds were listening. There wasn't much to say, but I got close enough to see the look in Jimmy's eyes, which betrayed his confident smile. What I saw was the glassy stare of a lifer looking at an endless stream of colorless days and the tedium of a clock that never seemed to move. He was a beaten man. And he and I both knew it.

With Jimmy out of the picture, the feds were a bit more willing to wheel and deal, caucusing regularly with our defense team. With Jack Stricklin squarely in their sights, their final offer was ten years for Jack, five years for everyone else. Had it been five and three, we might have considered it. But we held out, knowing we would likely get the same deal from a jury.

The trial itself was a three-week lesson in civics, impressively staged in the "Big Room," an imposing marble and mahogany tribunal with ceilings that soared and windows that overlooked downtown Boston. Impressively seated high on his bench was Federal District Judge Walter Skinner, a man described by the *New York Times* as "a tough old Yankee who ran his court with a sense of humor." They were right on the money. Judge Skinner was everything you could ask for in a judge—fair, impartial and totally human in his approach to the job. He wasn't a deity ruling from on high. He was a hard-working jurist, splitting his docket to handle two cases at a time. We got the morning shift.

The case against us was iron clad. The Government put on a thoroughly convincing prosecution, with both Scott Emlong and Dan Cacy relating the story of Folly Cove in complete and compelling detail. What the Government didn't know, they made up. What they couldn't make up, they lied about. They had names and dates, pictures, charts, records, and graphs. They brought people in to identify us in court that we had never laid eyes on. They weren't taking any chances of losing out on a twenty-nine ton bust, even if it was five years after the fact. It took them the better part of three weeks to present their evidence. The jury was convinced of our guilt within the first three minutes.

At the head of the defense team was a crusty trial lawyer from Midland/Odessa named Warren Burnett. To his peers, Warren ranked right up there with Percy Foreman and Racehorse Haynes. He was a disheveled dynamo who appeared in court wearing the same rumpled blue corduroy suit every day. He would approach the witness looking like an unmade bed. But when he spoke, he dominated the scene in a way that demanded your full attention.

Warren Burnett may have been a harmless looking curmudgeon, but if you were in his crosshairs, you could only react in helpless horror as he proceeded to cut your throat. Judge Skinner lauded him openly (but never within earshot of the jury), naming him the best he had ever seen at the art of cross-examination. The jury ate him up. But not even the impressive skills of Warren Burnett were enough to overcome the obvious flaw in our case.

When the Government rested, and it was time at last to present our defense, we knew we were well and truly fucked. We did it. And they all knew we did it. Our only option would be to lie under oath. We knew the Government had withheld evidence. It never came out in court, for instance, that I, or anyone else, had purchased a vehicle in the area. The prosecution was way too thorough to have overlooked such an obvious detail. They were licking their chops to get us on the stand and pile perjury on top of perjury. Our lawyers strongly advised us not to testify. So we put it in the hands of the jury and prayed for lenience.

Though we knew we had lost the case, we were clinging to the hope that we had won the jury. Throughout the trial, they had appeared far less outraged than amused. The Judge himself could hardly keep from laughing out loud on several occasions. Never once in the entire three weeks did he refer to our conspiracy as a crime. He called it an adventure, a caper, an escapade, a scam—but never a crime. And Warren Burnett had done such a masterful job laying waste to the snitches, the jury held them in higher contempt than any of us. As the trial progressed, they began to see us with less and less derision and more and more curiosity. We clung to our hope, but we knew it was a long shot.

On the morning we were to open and rest our defense, Judge Skinner unexpectedly excused the jury and curtly announced to the court that he had heard enough. The facts were all too clear. It was time to conclude the proceedings.

We squirmed uncomfortably in our seats, wondering if we were about to go to jail right then and there. Even our attorneys seemed ill at ease. Suddenly, straight out of the corner in deep left field, Judge Skinner sternly faced the prosecution table and said, "Gentlemen, it's time to make a deal."

"But, Your Honor," answered the feds. "We've already offered them a deal, and they turned it down."

"In that case," replied the Judge, "offer them a better one."

We waved our right to a trial by jury and deferred to the Judge, who immediately found us guilty. Jack Stricklin, who was landing airplanes during the entire trial, would be apologetically sentenced to four months at the institution of his choosing. The rest of us would receive three years probation. Such is the difference geography makes. Had we been tried in Texas, a five-year prison sentence would have been the minimum. Jack would have gotten ten.

Love ya', Boston.

As part of the pre-sentencing ritual that followed our 1980 Boston conviction, we were each required to submit for the record a "Defendant's Version of the Crime," a chronicle of what we had done, an accounting of what we had learned. Extra credit would be awarded for sufficient remorse. My effort, needless to say, left a good deal to be desired. In fact, what I have come to regret most after all this time is the extent to which I shortchanged the court in my original document.

So now, after more than forty years to ruminate—and with the help of friends—I hereby amend my statement to the court.

Why? Because the young have time and the old have stories. And good ones deserve to be shared.

The preceding is true. The events are documented, and the characters are real. This is how a small brotherhood of once-errant stoners chased a life-altering high in pursuit of the largest load of Colombian pot that had yet to reach our shores. A lot of people got high, a few people got rich, and nobody got hurt. As far as we were concerned, we broke a law that was already broken.

Marijuana is the human equivalent of catnip—the perfect antidote to the speed of life. Its effects are less harmful than a bag of groceries. And you can grow it in a closet. It has become the high of choice for millions of otherwise law-abiding users. And the only harmful side effects are those administered by the U.S Department of Justice.

Pot is not the problem. And putting people in jail for its use is not the solution. If we had dealt with it fairly in the first place, that juicy bud would be just another bottle of wine—amusing but not overbearing with complex undertones of sun and sky. Big business would embrace it like a rich uncle. And big government would tax it to the heavens. But instead, pot remains relegated to, "That's some good shit, bro. How much for a lid?"

So users become dealers. Dealers become informers. Lawyers become rich. Jails become full. And Uncle Sam becomes more and more committed to swinging a sledgehammer at a thumbtack. How many billions of dollars must we spend to enforce a law that is as ineffective as it is unnecessary?

I will end my statement to the court with the admission that after humping the shit out of 58,000 pounds of primo Colombian during three adrenaline-fueled nights on the coast of Massachusetts, I am troubled only by the chronically painful regret of a screaming lower lumbar. An illicit toke or two in the evening helps dull the pain and remains the ideal way to savor the passing of another day—the organic remedy for a restless mind and the perfect way to laugh, to live, and to never take yourself more seriously than a fart in the wind.

EPILOGUE

Lee Chagra would be shot to death during a robbery of his downtown El Paso law office on New Year's Eve 1978. During the investigation, the DEA swept in and harvested a wealth of information, abandoning any pretense of attorney-client privilege. The evidence they collected led to a string of successful prosecutions, but did little to advance the notion of Lee as a kingpin.

As to the murder itself, conjecture included everything from an angry cartel to a Mafia hit to a Government-sponsored assassination. But in the end, it turned out to be nothing more than a robbery gone tragically wrong.

Lee Chagra was one of the great characters of the '70s drug wars—a charismatic attorney with the style of a riverboat gambler and the reputation of a cobra. The Government would never prove a single crime against him. It would cost millions of dollars and take nearly ten years to finally convince the United States attorneys that they had the wrong Chagra.

Though the government failed to convict Jimmy Chagra of the murder of Judge Wood, Jimmy would be buried in the federal correctional system for more than twenty years. Ultimately, he would convince the authorities that he had something to offer. As to the level of his cooperation, I have no idea. But it was enough to land him in the relative comfort of protective custody, ultimately to enter witness protection and be relocated somewhere far away from the legions of past associates who would wish him harm.

Not even the fear of fatal retribution prevented Jimmy from trying to get back in the game. He stayed in touch with old friends, none of them crazy enough to do business with him. He and Jack Stricklin occasionally spoke by phone until Jimmy's death from brain cancer in 2008. As he told Jack in what would be their final conversation, "Brother, if there is a hell, I know I'm going there."

After the Boston deal, Billy Russell fulfilled his twenty-one month Roswell obligation at La Tuna. He would be out of prison less than a day before making a new connection in the halfway house—a guy who would eventually lead him to the *two Rafas*, a pair of unrelated Mexican car thieves named Rafael who had connections in the fields, but no significant buyers. Billy would amend that scenario in short order.

They began with carloads, graduated to vans, and ended up filling semi-trucks. Over the course of a few years, the Rafas literally took ownership of the International Bridge, never once losing a load. Billy, meanwhile, created a nationwide distribution network that ran with precision and left the footprint of a butterfly. He became one of the border's most successful importers, without so much as a passing glance from the DEA.

Billy Russell was smart enough to know that sooner or later everyone gets busted. Getting out of the pot business, however, proved nearly as difficult as getting in. He retired often, devoting himself to a newly acquired cabinet company, which operated for a time as a maquiladora, manufacturing in Mexico, and trucking across the bridge for distribution. It was a game he knew how to play. And he might have finally been content to play it for the rest of his life had it not been for the persuasive abilities of a certain snitch.

Ultimately, he would be indicted for a minor role in a tangled conspiracy—a vague medley of transactions with which he had absolutely no involvement. He was guilty, of course, of an entirely different collection of felonies. And with priors for Roswell and Boston already in his jacket, it was his third strike—enough to earn him fifteen years in federal custody.

Billy would battle cancer as an inmate of a federal correctional institution, which is to say he would battle a federal correctional institution. It was poorly staffed, ill equipped, and largely unmotivated to deal with even the most basic treatment. Billy Russell was in for a stretch he did not expect to outlive. But fate intervened.

During the trial, Billy was one of multiple defendants, each with his own lawyer. It was a judicial clusterfuck that so befuddled the jury, they issued a blanket conviction and let the judge sort it out from there. But in all the confusion, no one seemed to notice when Billy's lawyer came down with a case of the flu and failed to show up in court for several days. It was a big enough breech to see his conviction tossed by the appellate court. Ultimately, the Government declined to re-prosecute. And the Billy Russell who walked out of prison after three years—and into the waiting arms of his wife, Sylvia—needed no further sign that it was time to return to the old straight and narrow.

After a lifetime spent in quest of total control, Billy Russell put himself in the hands of a higher power and achieved a level of serenity that sustains him to this day. Everything happens for a reason, he believes. Billy was spared having to spend the rest of his life in prison, and his cancer went into remission. It was a blessing he did not intend to waste.

Today Billy is known to preach a sermon now and then. He has helped build a church and ministered to the homeless. And he tends to his vegetable garden with the devotion of a monk. Billy Russell continues to live his life in a straightforward direction, embracing every day with a total commitment to the righteous cause of a merciful God and a life well lived.

Prior to beginning the book, I never really knew Ralph Armendariz. I knew the mechanics of his role, but he was in and out of my life so fast we hardly got acquainted. The telling of our tale, though, has kindled the bond of Boston. And we have become friends, talking often by phone and keeping up with each other's ills and issues.

Ralph would ultimately answer for his role in the Folly Cove conspiracy. Being savvy enough to insist the matter be settled in a Boston court, he would receive probation like the rest of us. But he stayed in the business and wound up serving five years on the runaway tongue of yet another talkative snitch. It was enough time to convince him that freedom is too big a price to pay.

Ralph kept up with his union dues for over forty years and continues to work as a respected member of the International Association of Heat and Frost Insulators and Allied Workers— the same union from which his father had retired. Happily, Ralph and his father bonded in adulthood and enjoyed a close relationship until the end. The values instilled through tough love continue to resonate as Ralph plies his trade, relishes his family, and pursues his faith.

Like everyone else involved, the summer of 1975 remains a vivid memory to Ralph Armendariz. Unlike everyone else, his memories are singular in perspective. The tale of his heroic journey was his alone to tell. And believe it or not, prior to writing the book, none of us had ever heard his whole story. Likewise, Ralph learned things he never knew about the Boston side of the deal. So forty years later, the story is finally complete.

"It's a story I've always wanted to tell," Ralph admitted. "If I had to do it all over again, I'd go back in minute. But I would ask for a lot more money."

Mike Halliday ended up doing a total of eleven and a half years in prison. Along the way he spent four years on the run as a federal fugitive and racked up a roster of felonies, most of which involved pot.

Mike was a smuggler—that's what he knew, that's what he

loved. Doing time was just part of the job. When the bill came due, he would construct his life on the inside as close as he could to his life on the outside. He made himself useful in prison. If you needed something, Mike Halliday was the go-to guy. If he couldn't smuggle it in, he'd build it. If it were broken, he'd fix it. And if you wanted to hide it, he could make it invisible. He was even known to apply a few stitches to various and sundry stab wounds. Mike made the most of his time in prison, expanding his intellect and refining his endless ideas. The walls may have contained his body, but his mind would never dance the Institutional Hop.

Like everyone else when the talk turns to glory days, Mike exhales not a single breath of regret—not for the crimes he committed or the time he served. He was chasing a high that took him places he never expected to go. He saw the view from the mountaintop and tasted the bitter lonesome of confinement. But he's still the kid who leads with his chin and dives headfirst into uncertain waters. He's still the kid who can't wait to take it apart so he can put it back together even better than it was.

Today, Mike devotes himself to the care of his beloved Betty, who taught him how to love and be loved. His incessant curiosity and analytical dexterity continue to feed a curious mind. From his theories on the treatment of cancer, to his views of the geo-political landscape, to his patented skylights, Mike will always worship at Our Lady of the Perpetual Brainstorm. He's the mad scientist who lives a simple life in constant wonder and eternal fascination. That's Mike—still tinkering after all these years.

MIKE HALLIDAY

> I always wanted to leave this world having done more good than harm. I believe that the only reason our government would hate and fear marijuana so much is because it gets people thinking. God did not put this wonderful plant on earth just to help fill the prisons.
>
> We didn't know it at the time and in truth it wasn't

our goal, but we probably did as much to end the war in Vietnam as anyone. After all, it was those pot-smoking hippies getting the shit kicked out of them every night on the news that finally brought it to an end.

I'm happy the story is finally being told. The hardest part has been keeping it short—there was too much going on to tell it all. I'd like to thank everyone who reads this—whatever thoughts you come away with—that's your right. Hopefully a day will come when we all have the right to do and think as we please as long as no other person is hurt.

I did what I did. I paid for it in full. And I'm at peace with everything that happened. I can't say it was the life I saw myself living. But I wouldn't trade the memories for anything.

Peace be with you.

I recently heard a memorable quote on a PBS Frontline episode that examined our penal system. They were interviewing the warden of a large federal institution, and he spoke of overcrowding and the abundance of non-violent criminals. "The Government," he said, "needs to decide exactly who it is they're mad at. And who it is they're afraid of."

The Government was clearly mad at Jack Stricklin. The marijuana leaf at the bottom of his pool only widened the target on his back. Many of those with whom he had previously done business were reluctant to even go near him. But Jack couldn't have gotten out of the business if he'd wanted to. And he didn't. He stayed in and continued to ride the highs and lows of the life he chose. Jack would never again know the success of Boston. But he did what he loved to do, and when it was time to pay the price, he paid it without compromise.

Jack Stricklin

Before he was killed, I was told by Lee Chagra that I was the first person to ever be indicted in a marijuana case under the CCE Act, Continuing Criminal Enterprise. It's called an 848—The Kingpin Statute.

The second time I was in La Tuna, these two agents came and pulled me into a room to be interviewed. They said, "Look, we're getting ready to indict you on a CCE, which means a life sentence. Do you really want to spend the rest of your life in jail? Help us out, and we'll give you money and a new identity. You can start over."

I didn't say a word.

And he said, "Just give us Lee Chagra, and we'll make sure you're outta here in six months with a clean slate. Just think about it—you don't want to spend the rest of your life in jail."

Then he took a card out of his pocket and said, "I'm going to put my home phone number on this so you can call me at home. If you think about this at midnight, you go get somebody, and they'll call me for you. You take this card." And he handed it to me across a conference table.

When I didn't reach out to take it, he put it down right in front of me. I said, "If I gave you Lee Chagra, I'd have to be two things I hate the most—a snitch and a liar. Lee Chagra is not guilty of anything but being a fucking lawyer. If you want to charge him with that, I'll testify. Otherwise, you can take that card and shove it up your ass."

For crimes related only to marijuana, Jack Stricklin would spend a combined total of twenty-four years in federal custody, his final sentence netting more than seventeen consecutive years as the Government made good on their threat to prosecute him as a kingpin. He likely could have won his release in less than half that time. But Jack held out until there was no one left to incriminate.

I visited Jack several times while he was in prison and received the occasional phone call. Never once did I come away feeling that he was beaten. I always found the same Jack I had known since I was twelve years old—upbeat and ready to share a laugh. Of course, visits and phone calls are special things to inmates. I'm certain there were dark times and profound regrets. But Jack was determined not to show it. And even more determined not to allow it to claim his self-respect.

Jack was close to sixty-five when he was finally released into a world transformed by the digital revolution. To this day, he struggles with anything more complicated than a tongue depressor. But he isn't bitter or angry, doesn't dwell on the past. In fact, given the chance he would do it all again. He paid in full with twenty-four years of his life and walked away with his integrity in his pocket.

Whenever Jack and I get together, it's as if I had seen him only yesterday. The years have exacted their toll on both of us, but Jack somehow managed to hang on to the twinkle in his eye, the ready sense of humor, and the rebellious spirit that defined him. He was an outlaw but never a criminal, a convict but never a con. He remains a man in the company of friends. And he remains a man who will never stop chasing his next big high.

I recently returned to El Paso for the happy occasion of Jack Stricklin's marriage to Elvia, the new love of his life. Mike Halliday was there, along with others in the crew. Johnny Milliorn died of cancer in 2013. His brother Jimmy died several years earlier. But enough of us were still around to spark a lively reunion—or as lively as it gets when you're looking at the far side of sixty.

It was a simple backyard ceremony with close friends and family. There were few in attendance that hadn't shared, in one way or another, the unlikely pursuits of Jack Stricklin. Billy Russell presided over the late afternoon ceremony and was far more nervous than the bride. But he pulled it off with the personal touch of a lifelong friend, enriching the vows with his spiritual presence.

Though Elvia saw to the ceremony, it was an event that perfectly reflected the style of Jack Stricklin—no fuss, no muss, let's party. And he couldn't have picked a better place. Following the wedding, he and Elvia invited everyone to be their guest at Ardovino's Desert Crossing, a family restaurant with a long-standing reputation for great Italian food in a unique Southwestern setting. A bit off the beaten path, Ardovino's sits alone atop a small bluff on the western edge of the Rio Grande Valley.

We held forth on a private patio overlooking the river and Old Mexico to the south. What better location to celebrate a new beginning. We were back where it started over forty years ago—on the edge of an arbitrary divide separating two countries

L to R: Bill Russell, Mike Halliday and Jack Stricklin, together again in 2016.

defined by a single culture. Not quite Mexico, not exactly Texas. But la frontera, where the law is what you make it, and opportunity is where you find it.

Fortified by good food and strong drink, one story led to another as laughter echoed off the sunset and into the evening. We relived our unlikely adventure and rekindled a bond that has held strong for more than forty years. As if the memories of our brief time together had been folded up and put in a drawer for just such an occasion, we unpacked our best days, when each of us in our own way had felt most alive.

For me, the reconnection with my borderland roots reignited a spark I had believed to be long ago extinguished. But the border never fully lets you go. It still holds claim to the piece of my soul that refused to accept the flawed doctrine of a corrupt government. The cause of cannabis has been pursued to a stalemate over decades of violence and waste. But for that brief window of time in the '70s, it was a benign crusade, waged by a brotherhood of outlaws who lived for the adrenaline and shared the righteous belief that if there is no harm, there is no foul.

And if I needed a further reminder of the high we chased from Mexico to Boston, I had only to look up on the hillside where agents of the U.S. Border Patrol were scanning the horizon with binoculars, in search of the human traffic they were duty-bound to curtail. I wished them little success in their efforts, while at the same time acknowledging that, just like us, they were tilting at windmills they had no hope of defeating. Just like us, they were secure in their virtue. And just like us, they were chasing a high all their own.

FINITO

ACKNOWLEDGMENTS

To my son Alex, who devoured this story in a single sitting and gave me the best review I could ever hope for.

To my sister Jesse, who lived the adventure from beginning to end. Without you, I never would have had a story to tell.

To Jennifer and Bryan, whose perception and enthusiasm lent needed direction to a wandering manuscript.

To Robert Boswell. You were at the table when it all began. I will forever be grateful for your generous and insightful contribution.

To my second family at the ad agency. Thanks to Rusty Haggard for his Photoshop expertise; to Brent Kaluikauha, Pablo Rossy and Joel Lamascus for pitching in on the layout. Thanks also to Tasha Hayes and Bill Meeder, early readers who let me know I had a story worth telling. To John Dufhilo and Kevin Brown, whose enthusiastic reviews of a later version propelled me to the finish line.

And special thanks to Scott Crum, a dear friend, amazing art director and atrocious speller who designed the cover and has been making my words look better than they are for nearly thirty years.

To Lee, Bobby and John Byrd of Cinco Puntos Press. Thanks for believing in the book and allowing me to be part of the process.

Finally, thank you, brother David. I never would have begun this project without your support. And I never would have finished it without your guidance and encouragement.